MAKING CONNECTIONS 3:

An Integrated Approach to Learning English

Carolyn Kessler

Jean Bernard-Johnston

Linda Lee

Mary Lou McCloskey

Mary Ellen Quinn

Lydia Stack

Heinle & Heinle Publishers
A Division of International Thomson Publishing, Inc.
Boston, MA 02116, U.S.A.

I(T)P

▲▲▲

The publication of *Making Connections* was directed by the members of the Heinle & Heinle Secondary ESL Publishing Team:

Editorial Director: Roseanne Mendoza
Senior Production Services Coordinator: Lisa McLaughlin
Market Development Director: Ingrid Greenberg
Developmental Editor: Nancy Jordan

Also Participating in the publication of this program were:

Publisher: Stan Galek
Director of Production: Elizabeth Holthaus
Senior Assistant Editor: Sally Conover
Manufacturing Coordinator: Mary Beth Hennebury
Composition: GTS Graphics
Project Management: GTS Graphics
Interior Design: Martucci Studio
Illustration: Jerry Malone/Martucci Studio
Cover Design: Martucci Studio

Manufactured in the United States of America

ISBN: 0-8384-3841-5

Heinle & Heinle Publishers is an International Thomson Publishing Company

10   9   8

$\mathscr{P}$REFACE

Middle and High School ESOL (English for Speakers of Other Languages) students are faced with a formidable task. In the few short years of school that remain, they must learn both English and the challenging content of their academic curriculum, made more challenging because so much language acquisition is demanded. *Making Connections: An Integrated Approach to Learning English* provides resources to integrate the teaching and learning of language and academic content. These resources help teachers and students develop students' ability to communicate in English as they focus on motivating themes with topics, activities, tools, and procedures that introduce the content areas of science, social studies, and literature.

Making Connections: An Integrated Approach to Learning English is designed to help secondary students and their teachers reach toward important, essential goals and to facilitate their learning language and content in the ways they learn best. What are the goals we reach for?

Joy—the joy in life and learning that will make our students happy, successful lifetime learners

Literacy—the ability to use reading and writing to accomplish amazing things

Community—the knowledge that they live in an accepting community where they have rights, responsibilities, and resources

Access—access to whatever resources they need to accomplish their own goals, including access to technology

Power—the power to make their lives into whatever they choose

What are the ways of teaching and learning that work best, according to our understanding of language acquisition research? The answer, we believe, is through **integrated learning.** *Making Connections* includes four different kinds of integration: language areas, language and academic content, students with one another, and school with the larger community.

- We integrate language areas through active learning.

We combine reading, writing, listening, and speaking into things that students **do.** Through interaction with authentic and culturally relevant literature, through activities that involve genuine communication, and through student-owned process writing, students learn the "parts" or "skills" of language in meaningful "whole" contexts.

- We integrate language with academic content and processes.

▲▲▲

Language is best learned when it is used as a tool, when students are meaningfully engaged in something important to them. Learning the language and participating in processes specific to the academic content area subjects are essential for preparing students to move into mainstream content-area classrooms. By teaching language through content, we attempt to do several things at once: we help students to learn to use a variety of learning strategies; introduce them to science, social studies and literature content appropriate for their age and grade levels; and help them to use accessible language and learn new esential language in the process.

■ We integrate students with one another.

We help teachers and students develop a real learning community in which students and teacher use a variety of strategies—including many cooperative learning strategies—to accomplish student-owned educational goals. We acknowledge that students are not all at the same level linguistically or academically but recognize that each student has strengths to offer in your classroom, so we provide choices of materials and activities that accommodate a multi-level class.

■ We integrate school with home culture and with the greater community.

We strive for materials and activities that are relevant for a culturally diverse group and that help students to develop their self-esteem by valuing their unique cultural heritages. We seek to involve students in the community and the community with schools by providing and encouraging activities and projects that relate to community life and that put students into interaction with community presentatives. This active involvement is integral to the development of students' content-area knowledge and language.

In order to reach toward these goals and implement these four kinds of integration, we have used integrated thematic units as the organizational basis for *Making Connections*. Our themes are arrived at in a variety of ways: some, like "Choosing Foods," have very concrete connections among the sections of the units. Others, like "Making Waves," make more metaphorical connections among sections that treat very different aspects of the theme. In all the units, students will make connections across content areas and will revisit themes and use and re-use the language of themes in different ways. Each unit provides multi-level information and experiences that integrate language with one or more content areas and includes the following features:

Learning strategies. In each unit, we incorporate strategies to help students with their language and content area learning. We encourage teachers and students to be aware of the applicability of these strategies in new learning situations. Our goal is to create active, capable, self-starting learners.

Cooperative learning. Cooperative learning has been shown to be effective in facilitating both student learning and successful cross-cultural, multi-level student integration. Each unit uses a variety of cooperative groupings and activities to achieve these goals.

Language Focus. Language is learned best in a meaningful, useful context. In *Making Connections,* students use language to accomplish real tasks, many of which they have chosen themselves from activity menus. From these meaningful contexts, many opportunities arise to teach language concepts as they are needed. Both the student text and the teacher's edition contain suggestions for taking advantage of opportunities for teaching language features as these opportunities arise.

Content-area experiences in science, social studies, and literature. We have chosen three content areas for focus in *Making Connections* because of their importance to student success and because of the importance of language to success in these areas. In science, we introduce the language of science (and frequently mathematics language as well) through offering authentic scientific experiences using materials that are accessible to an ESOL teacher. In social studies, we take advantage of the multicultural nature of ESOL classes to introduce the processes of the social sciences. We have provided literature in a variety of genres to enhance content-area learning. As students begin to learn the language, they need to talk about and create their own literary works.

Choices for teachers and students in multicultural, multilevel classrooms. Every ESOL class is a multilevel, multicultural class. In order to meet the needs of these diverse groups and in order to empower both teachers and students, *Making Connections* offers many choices. Teachers can choose among the many activities in the units to provide experiences most appropriate to their classes and can sequence these activities as needed. They can also individualize by choosing different activities for different students within the class. Each unit includes an activity menu of experiences and projects that will help students to integrate and apply the material from the unit. Both teacher and students can make choices among these culminating events to suit them to student interests, level of ability, and needs. Related literary selections following each unit offer additional choices for teachers and students interested in reading extensions.

Since we are teachers as well as authors, we know that the most important aspect of your instructional program is what happens between teacher and student. We have tried to develop a program that offers teachers and students many choices of activities, resources, and ideas that provide chances to interact, learn, and grow. We hope *Making Connections* helps students learn what they need to experience success in school as well as in life. We welcome teacher feedback and students' responses to *Making Connections.*

The authors

CONTENTS

Study Strategies	Reading Selections

Quickwriting
Predicting
Taking Notes
Previewing
Using Context
Making a Time Line
Classifying
Listening for Specific
   Information
	The Waves of Matsuyama (Japanese *tanka* by Saigyo)
	Excerpt from The Sea Around Us (by Rachel Carson)
	Earth Shaker, Wave Maker (a Greek myth)
	Letter from a Dutch Immigrant, 1846
	An Oral History (by Saverio Rizzo)
	Could We Ever Forget? (a poem by Ok Kork)
	My Name is Monique . . . (excerpt from personal essay
	   by Monique Rubio)
	How Everything Happens (a poem by May Swenson)
	At the Beach (a poem by Kemal Ozer)
	The Education of Berenice Belizaire (from a magazine article
	   by Joe Klein)
	Song for Smooth Waters (a Native American poem)
	West Side (a poem by Naomi Shihab Nye)

Brainstorming
Previewing
Making a Tree Diagram
Using Context
Predicting
Making a Story Map
Using Context
Brainstorming
	Who's Hu? (a short story by Lensey Namioka)
	Nicholasa Mohr (an autobiographical account)
	The Underground Railroad (a magazine article by
	   Robert W. Peterson)
	The Douglass "Station" of the Underground Railroad (a play by
	   Glennette Tilley Turner)
	The Road Not Taken (a poem by Robert Frost)
	Jessica Berg (a poem by Mel Glenn)
	Footpath (a poem by Stella Ngatho)
	Harriet Tubman (a poem by Eloise Greenfield)

Classifying Previewing Using Context Using Context Brainstorming Quickwriting Taking Notes in a Chart Brainstorming Previewing	Zoo (a short story by Edward Hoch) Breaking Mental Barriers (a magazine article) A Shameful Chapter (a book excerpt by Barbara Rogasky) In Reponse to Executive Order 9066 (a poem by Dwight Okita) Aiming for Peace (a magazine article by Scott Brodeur) As I Grew Older (a poem by Langston Hughes) Those Who Don't (a poem by Sandra Cisneros)

Brainstorming
Listening for Specific
   Information
Making a Web Diagram
Taking Notes in a Chart
	Far, Far Away She Was Going (excerpt from the *Kim Van Kieu*)
	The Old Man at the Bridge (a short story by Ernest Hemingway)
	I Felt Like a Queen (a memoir by Suzanne Flores)
	You've Got a Friend (a song by Carole King)
	Letter to My Sister Who Lives in a Foreign Land (a poem
	   by Daisy Zamora)
	Across Ages (a magazine article by Scott Brodeur)
	August 2002: Night Meeting (from *The Martian Chronicles,*
	   by Ray Bradbury)
	The Eighth Wonder of the World (historical overview)
	Poetry of Friendship (a poem by José Marti)

$\mathcal{A}$CKNOWLEDGMENTS

The authors want to thank colleagues, students, and teachers from whom we have learned much and who have offered strong and encouraging support for this project. We thank Chris Foley, Roseanne Mendoza, Nancy Mann, Elaine Leary, and Lisa McLaughlin for their support in the development and production of this project and for weathering with us the storms and challenges of doing something so new. We also want to thank family members—Erin, Dierdre, and Jim Stack; Kevin and Sean O'Brien, and Joel and Tom Reed; Alysoun, Eliot, and Mike Johnston—for their love and support during this project.

The publisher and authors wish to thank the following teachers who pilot tested the *Making Connections* program. Their valuable feedback on teaching with these materials greatly improved the final product. We are grateful to all of them for their dedication and commitment to teaching with the program in a prepublication format.

Elias S. Andrade and Gudrun Draper
James Monroe High School
North Hills, CA

Nadine Bagel
Benjamin Franklin Middle School
San Francisco, CA

Kate Bamberg
Newcomer High School
San Francisco, CA

David Barker and Carolyn Bohlman
Maine Township High School East
Park Ridge, IL

Kate Charles
Sycamore Junior High School
Anaheim, CA

Efrain Diaz
Collier County Public Schools
Naples, FL

Anne Elmkies, Irene Killian, and Kay Stark
Hartford Public Schools
Hartford, CT

Genoveva Goss
Alhambra High School
Alhambra, CA

Margaret Hartman
Lewisville High School
Lewisville, TX

Carmen N. Jimenez
Intermediate School 184
New York, NY

Rob Lamont and Judith D. Clark
Trimble Technical High School
Fort Worth, TX

Judi Levin
Northridge Middle School
Northridge, CA

Ligita Longo
Spring Woods High School
Houston, TX

Mary Makena
Rancho Alamitas High School
Garden Grove, CA

Alexandra M. McHugh
Granby, CT

Beatrice W. Miranda
Leal Middle School
San Antonio, TX

Doris Partan
Longfellow School
Cambridge, MA

Jane Pierce
Douglas MacArthur High School
San Antonio, TX

Cynthia Prindle
Thomas Jefferson High School
San Antonio, TX

Sydney Rodrigues
Doig Intermediate School
Garden Grove, CA

Cecelia Ryan
Monte Vista High School
Spring Valley, CA

Patsy Thompson
Gwinnett Vocational Center
Lawrenceville, GA

Fran Venezia
North Dallas High School
Dallas, TX

The publisher and authors would also like
to thank the following people who reviewed
the *Making Connections* program at various
stages of development. Their insights and
suggestions are much appreciated.

Irene Papoulis
Institute for Writing and Thinking
Bard College
Annandale-on-Hudson, NY

Suzanne Barton
Fort Worth Independent School District
Fort Worth, TX

Keith Buchanan
Fairfax County Public Schools
Fairfax, VA

Carlos Byfield
San Diego City College
San Diego, CA

John Croes
Lowell High School
Lowell, MA

Flo Decker
El Paso, TX

Lynn Dehart
North Dallas High School
Dallas, TX

Cecelia Esquer
El Monte High School
El Monte, CA

Marge Gianelli
Canutillo Independent School District
El Paso, TX

Nora Harris
Harlandale Independent School District
San Antonio, TX

Richard Hurst
Holbrook High School
Holbrook, AZ

Betty J. Mace-Matluck
Southwest Educational Development
  Laboratory
Austin, TX

Jacqueline Moase-Burke
Oakland Independent School District
Oakland, MI

Jeanne Perrin
Boston Public Schools
Boston, MA

Ron Reese
Long Beach Unified School District
Long Beach, CA

Linda Sasser
Alhambra School District
Alhambra, CA

Donna Sievers
Garden Grove Unified School District
Garden Grove, CA

Stephen F. Sloan
James Monroe High School
North Hills, CA

Dorothy Taylor
Adult Learning Center
Buffalo Public Schools
Buffalo, NY

Beth Winningham
James Monroe High School
North Hills, CA

COMPONENTS OF THE MAKING CONNECTIONS PROGRAM

In addition to the student text, each level of Making Connections includes the following components:

Teacher's Extended Edition

This Teacher's Extended Edition provides:

- an introduction to the thematic, integrated teaching approach
- a description of several approaches to presenting literature selections
- a guide to the study strategies that appear in the student book
- detailed teaching suggestions for each activity
- suggestions for extension activities
- listening scripts

Workbooks

Workbooks provide additional practice in using the vocabulary, language functions, language structures, and study strategies introduced in each of the thematic units. Workbook activities can be used in class or assigned as homework.

CD-ROM

This lively, fun, user-friendly program features highly interactive units that parallel the student text. Students engage in sentence completion, interact with videos, create notes from a variety of sources, and complete graphs and charts. Also included is a writing area, an additional language practice section, and printing scorecards for each unit. The program is colorful, easy to navigate and offers a help feature on every screen.

Literacy Masters

Literacy Masters provide special support for preliterate students. These materials are designed for students who enter the program at the Preproduction or Early Production stage. (Students who have only minimal comprehension of English.) The materials correspond with the units of *Making Connections I* and are very useful in multilevel classes.

The Teacher's Guide to the Heinle & Heinle ESL Program

The Heinle & Heinle ESL Program consists of the two series: *Making Connections 1, 2, and 3*, and *Voices in literature, Bronze, Silver, and Gold*, which can be used independently or together. The Teacher's Guide th the Heinle & Heinle ESL Program provides much practical advice and strategies for using the two series together. In this guide, classroom practitioners will learn how to take advantage of the revisitation of terms, themes, content and literature are organized thematically, students can continuously relate and analyze academic concepts and literary works. This Teacher's Guide also offers strategies for providing instruction to students at many levels— from beginning English language proficiency to advanced levels of content-based and literature-based instruction. A technology section describes how instructors can use electronic support, such as e-mail and software, to expand on the activities found in *Making Connections* and *Voices in Literature*.

Assessment Program

The Assessment Program consists of several components and accommodates a range of assessment philosophies and formats. Included are:

- a portfolio assessment kit, complete with a teacher's guide to using portfolios and forms for student and teacher evaluation
- two "progress checks" per unit
- one comprehensive test per unit

Transparencies

Color Transparencies provide enlargements of visuals from the student texts. Many teachers find it helpful to view visuals with the students as they point out details. They may also write on pages using blank overlay transparencies.

Activity Masters

Reproducible activity masters support activities from the student book by providing write-on forms and graphic organizers for student's use. Activities for use with these masters consistently promote active student roles in engaging experiences.

Tape Program

Audio Tapes provide opportunities for group and individual extended practice with the series materials. The tapes contain all the listening activities included in the student texts. Scripts of the recorded material are included in the Teacher's Extended Edition.

▲▲▲

Unit 1:

MAKING WAVES

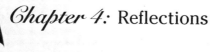

1

Chapter 1: What Makes Waves?

1. Share a Poem

a. Classwork. Look at the picture. Imagine yourself alone here. What sounds would you hear as you look at the waves? How would you feel?

b. Read the poem. What does it say about waves?

c. Why do you think the poet Saigyo wrote this poem?

The waves
of Matsuyama[1]
Their aspect[2] is unchanged
but of you, my lord[3]
no trace remains

Saigyo (1118-1190)

Matsuyamano
nami nokeshiki wa
kawaraji o
kaka naku kimi was
narimashinikeri

[1]Matsuyama   a city in northeastern Japan
[2]aspect   the way something looks
[3]my lord   the Emperor Suhoko

2. Explore

a. Look up the word "wave" in a dictionary. How many meanings does it have? Write the definition that fits the meaning of "waves" in the picture and the poem.

b. Read the other definitions. Which ones are new for you?

c. What do all waves have in common? Write a sentence that describes all of the different kinds of waves. Share your sentence with the class.

All waves _____

Study Strategy:

Quickwriting

See page 168.

3. Quickwrite

Imagine a lake or ocean in a storm. Think about a place you have been or have seen in a movie or photograph. Quickwrite about the scene for five minutes. What do the waves look like? What do they sound like? How do they make you feel?

4. Measure a Wave

Materials: *cotton rope, ruler, watch, piece of string*

Pairwork. Ask your partner to hold one end of the rope while you hold the other close to the floor. Pull the rope out tight close to the floor. While your partner holds his or her end of the rope still, shake your end back and forth. Experiment until you can make a regular pattern of waves with the rope on the floor. Then follow these steps to learn the speed of your wave.

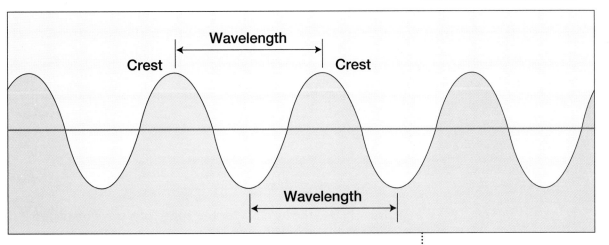

Step 1: Ask a classmate to use the ruler to measure the length of one of your waves. The **wavelength** is the distance between two high points (**crests**). Write the measurement of this wave in **centimeters (cm)** under Wave #1 in the chart.

Step 2: Tie a ribbon or piece of string around the middle of the rope. Invite a classmate to count how many waves pass the fixed point (where the string is) in ten seconds. Try it several times before you record the number.

Step 3: Divide the number you got in Step 2 by 10. This is the **frequency** of your wave. Write the frequency of Wave #1 in a chart like the one below.

Step 4: Use the following equation to find the speed of your wave: *speed = wavelength × frequency.*

Write the speed of Wave #1 in **centimeters per second (cm/s)** on the chart.

Study Strategy:

Predicting

See page 168.

	Wave #1	Wave #2
Wavelength		
Frequency		
Speed		

Step 5: What is the fastest wave you can make with the rope? Predict the speed.

Step 6: Use the rope to make the fastest possible wave. Then repeat steps 1 through 4 and add the information to the chart under Wave #2.

How close was your prediction about the speed of the wave?

Tell the class how you measured the rope waves and describe the results.

 5. **What's Missing?**

Pairwork. Use the formula for the speed of a wave on page 5 to complete a chart like this.

speed (v) in centimeters (cm)/second(s)	wavelength (l) in centimeters (cm)	frequency (f) in hertz (hz)
330 cm/s		300 hz
330 cm/s	2.5 cm	
50 cm/s		10 hz
100 cm/s	2.5 cm	
25 cm/s		5 hz

v = velocity   rate of motion in a specific direction
hz = hertz   a unit of frequency equal to one cycle per second

Describe each of the waves in this chart (fast, long, etc.)

 6. **Share Ideas**

Pairwork. What causes ocean waves? Think about each of the possible causes on the next list. Check (✓) the ones you think really can make waves. Add others if you wish. Discuss your choices with a partner. Feel free to agree or disagree.

A: I think the moon causes ocean waves.

B: Well, I don't think so. In my opinion, earthquakes are
the main cause.

CAUSE		EFFECT
_____ earthquakes		
_____ wind		
_____ rain		OCEAN WAVES
_____ the moon		
_____ lightning		

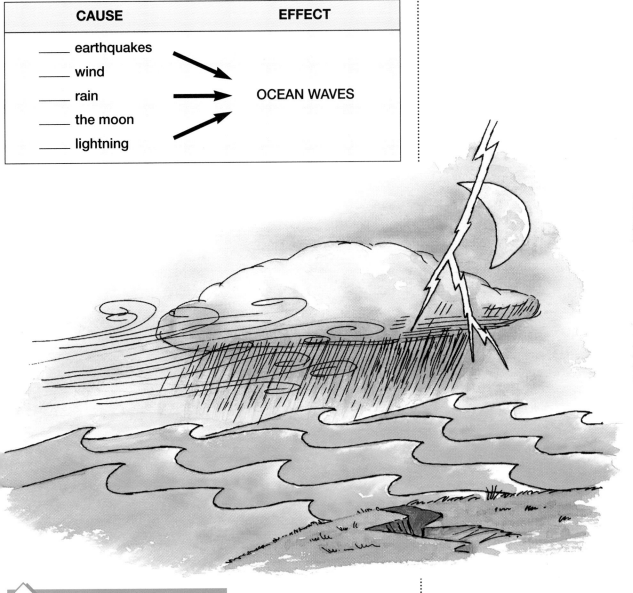

7. **Shared Reading**

On your own. Read the article and study the diagrams. Look for
information about the causes of ocean waves.

from
THE SEA AROUND US
by Rachel Carson

Wind is the great maker of waves. There are exceptions, such as the tidal waves sometimes produced by earthquakes under the sea. But the waves most of us know are produced by winds blowing over the sea.

Now, before constructing[1] an imaginary life history of a typical[2] wave, we need to know certain physical things about it. A wave has height, from trough to crest. It has length—the distance from its crest to that of the following wave. The period of the wave means the time it takes for succeeding[3] crests to pass a fixed point.

None of these things stays the same—for all depend upon the wind, upon the the depth of the water, and many other matters.

The water that makes up a wave does not advance[4] with it across the sea. Each particle of water turns around in a little circle or ellipse[5] with the passing of the wave, but returns very nearly to its original position. And it is fortunate that this is so. For if the huge masses of water that make up a wave actually moved across the sea, navigation[6] would be impossible.

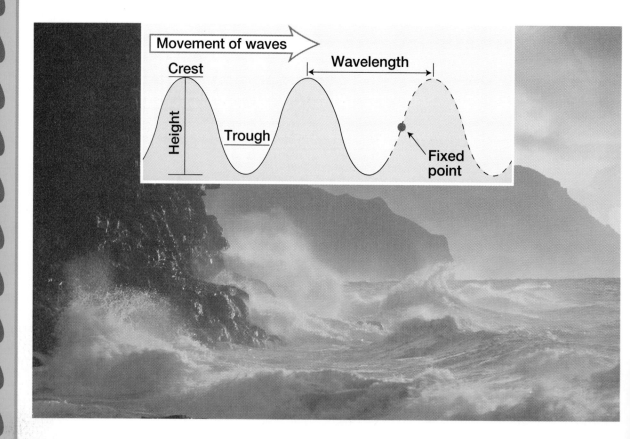

Let us look at a typical wave, born of wind and water far out in the Atlantic Ocean. Let us assume[7] that the wind is not so strong as to blow the top off and that the wave has merely grown to its full height. With its fellow waves it forms a confused, irregular pattern known as a "sea." Gradually as the waves pass out of the storm area, they lose height. The distance between crest and crest increases. The "sea" becomes a "swell," moving at an average speed of about 15 miles an hour.

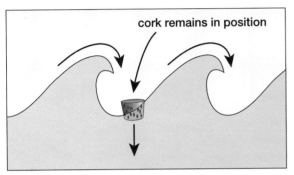

This cork will remain as the waves pass by.

Near the coast, the pattern becomes more orderly—a series of long, evenly spaced ridges.[8] But as the swell enters shallow water, a startling transformation takes place. For the first time in its life, the wave feels the drag of shoaling bottom.[9] Its speed slackens. Crests of following waves crowd in toward it. Abruptly[10] its height increases and the wave form steepens.[11] Then with a spilling, tumbling rush of water falling down into its trough, the wave dissolves in a seething[12] confusion of foam.

[1]**constructing**	building
[2]**typical**	normal
[3]**succeeding**	following, coming after
[4]**advance**	move ahead
[5]**ellipse**	a flattened circle
[6]**navigation**	to make a ship move in a certain direction
[7]**assume**	agree to be true
[8]**ridge**	long, narrow crest
[9]**a shoaling bottom**	a shallow area
[10]**abruptly**	suddenly
[11]**steepens**	gets higher
[12]**seething**	moving quickly, angrily

Rachel Carson (1907-1964)

After graduating from Johns Hopkins University, Rachel Carson began a long career as a marine biologist and writer. *The Sea Around Us* was published in 1951 and won the National Book Award. She was especially concerned about the dangers of environmental pollution. Her best known book, *The Silent Spring* (1962), helped raise awareness of this issue among readers around the world.

Study Strategy:

Taking Notes

See page 169.

8. Take Notes in a Chart

Pairwork. Look back at the reading and take notes in a chart like this one.

Paragraph	Topic What's the paragraph about?	Details and Examples
1	causes of ocean waves	-wind (main cause) -earthquakes (tidal waves)
2	physical characteristics	-height -
3	movement	
4		
5		

Language Focus:

Active and Passive Voice

Wind causes waves to form. Waves are caused by wind.

9. Test Your Knowledge

a. Pairwork. Get together with another pair. Take turns asking and answering questions about the information in your chart.

Example: Q: What causes waves?
A: Most waves are caused by wind blowing over the sea.

b. Discuss the information about waves in the reading. Here are some questions to think about.

What did you already know?
What new information surprised you?
What more would you like to learn?

10. Define

a. On your own. The following terms are used to describe waves. Use information from the reading and the diagrams to write a short definition of each one.

crest   length   period
trough   height   speed

b. Pairwork. Make a sketch that illustrates at least three of the terms you defined. Present your sketch to the class.

11. Analyze

Classwork. What effects do the following conditions have on the size and movement of a wave? List your ideas.

CAUSE	EFFECT
A storm blows up in the open sea.	_____ _____
The waves pass out of the storm area.	_____ _____
The swell enters shallow water near the shore.	_____ _____

12. Apply

Groupwork. Imagine you are the crew of a small sailboat on the open sea. You learn by radio that a storm with 15 ft. (4.6 m) waves is approaching your position at a speed of 10 miles (1.6 km) per hour. At this rate, you estimate that the storm will reach you in two hours. You are not certain you can get to the shore in that amount of time. You can already feel the wind blowing stronger and the sea beginning to swell. Choose one of these options (A or B) or suggest one of your own (C).

A. try to make it in to shore

B. stay out at sea and "ride out" the storm

C. _____

Discuss the possible dangers of each choice and reach a group decision. Explain your decision to the class.

Chapter 2: Ups and Downs

*W*aves can be relaxing, beautiful, exciting, or terrifying. Perhaps that is why people have often connected strong emotions such as love, joy, anger, or excitement with images of waves. In this section, you will read about some of these connections.

1. **Quickwrite**

a. Write for ten minutes without stopping. Describe a time in your life when you felt a wave of excitement or another strong emotion. You may want to think about these questions as you write.

- Where were you?
- Who was with you?
- What happened?
- What did you think or feel?

b. Share your story with a partner. Ask questions about your partner's story.

12

Study Strategy:

Previewing

See page 167.

2. Preview

Pairwork. Look at the photograph. Imagine how the surfer feels at this moment. What do you think he is saying to himself? Write down as many ideas as you can in a chart like the one below.

What we think the surfer is saying to himself	Did he really say this to himself?

3. Listening

Pairwork. Listen as a surfer describes his experience riding waves near Waimea, Hawaii. Check things on your list from #2 that are the same as or similar to things the surfer says. Which things were different?

4. Use Context

On your own. Guess the meaning of the italicized words from the story you just heard. Use the words and ideas in the sentence to help you decide.

You could see this *set* coming from way outside.	surfboard/series of waves
When you're in that situation there's this little voice inside you that's probably just a *vital instinct* talking saying, "okay, you better paddle for the horizon,"	desire to live/memory
So on about the fifth one I just *took some strokes* and hopped to my feet.	paddled fast/got sick
I could have taken one of the worst *wipeouts* of my life, but it turned out to be one of the best rides.	falls/prizes

---

Study Strategy:

Using Context

See page 169.

---

5. Role Play

Pairwork. Pretend you are a newspaper reporter while your partner takes the role of Richard Schmidt, the surfer whose story you just heard. You are on the beach just after Richard's ride on the "big one." Listen to the story again. Ask questions about his experience.

Reporter: How did you feel when you saw the set coming?
Richard: I felt really scared.

6. Evaluate

Classwork. Some people think that surfers like Richard Schmidt are cool, and other people think they are crazy. What do you think? State your opinion to the class. How many of the students in your class have tried surfing or would like to try it?

7. Write

a. On your own. Look back at your quickwriting from Step #1. See if you can remember more details about the experience. Make as many notes as you can in the observation chart.

b. Pairwork. Read your quickwriting aloud and show your chart to a partner. Invite your partner to ask questions about the experience. See if your partner can help you add more details to your observation chart.

c. On your own. Write a first draft about your experience. Use ideas from your quickwriting and your observation chart. For more suggestions about writing a first draft, see the Writer's Guide, page 173.

Groupwork. Read your story aloud to a small group of classmates. Ask your listeners to repeat their favorite sentences from your story and tell you what more they would like to know about your experience.

> **Language Focus:**
>
> **Sensory Verbs**
>
> It looked funny.
> I felt tired.
> The broccoli looked like a tree.
> The cat sounded like a baby.

Observation Chart: Remembering an Experience				
Sight	Sound	Feel	Taste	Smell

8. Preview

Classwork. Look at the map of ancient Greece. Why do you think the sea was important to the Greeks? What did their ships look like? How did the sailors feel about wind and waves? Explain what led you to your answers.

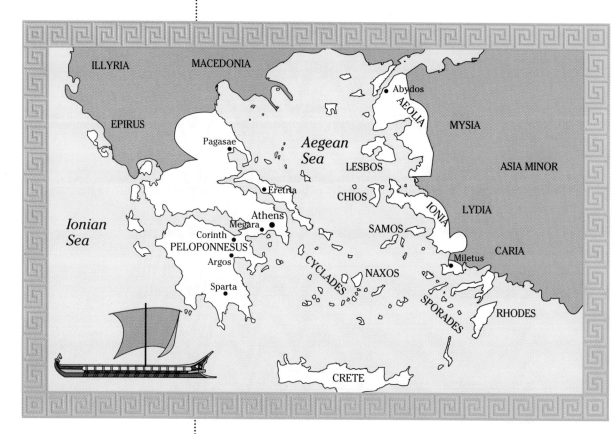

9. Shared Reading

Classwork. The ancient Greeks believed that waves and earthquakes were caused by Poseidon,[1] god of the sea. This story, based on the myth of Poseidon, is in the form of a play. Listen and read along.

[1]**Poseidon**   Neptune in Roman mythology

Earth Shaker, Wave Maker
The Myth of Poseidon

SCENE 1

(sound of lute music)

Bard: This story I will tell, of the all-powerful Poseidon, blue-haired lord of the sea, before whom all mortals tremble. You have heard many tales of his anger, his jealousy, his vengeance—how he stirs up a raging sea, how he shakes the earth when it pleases him—*(sound of waves)* but listeners—this is not a night for such fearful tales. Observe the dazzling stars, feel the gentle sea breeze. Tonight I will please you with a much more delightful story of the mighty Poseidon's gentler side; of his courtship of the delicate and beautiful Queen Amphritite. How did it begin?

(sound of waves, water increases, then subsides)

Poseidon: She has stolen my heart. I can think of nothing else. Observe, Dolphin! I am weak. I am no longer able to frighten sailors or terrify land dwellers. I must marry Amphritite!

Dolphin: But my Lord, she is terrified of you. She has run away.

Poseidon: *(beginning to anger)* She dares to flee mighty Poseidon? If she is within my watery realm, Dolphin, find her! Bring her here immediately!

Dolphin: I'm sorry, my lord. She has fled to the mountains, to the realm of Atlas for protection. He has granted her refuge in a lonely cave, with only birds for companions. She cannot be forced to do anything against her will, but perhaps she can be persuaded.

Poseidon: Then go to her, Dolphin. You are a creature of both water and air. Tell her of the glittering beauty of this undersea world. Tell her I will share this beautiful golden palace, and all of my power with her.

Dolphin: But, my lord. It is you and your power she fears.

Poseidon: Then convince her! Tell her of my incredible wealth, but not only that. Impress her with my generosity and deep respect for all creatures of the sea. After all, it is only outsiders who enrage me.

Dolphin: As you wish. But I can make no promises. She has a mind of her own, as you well know.

SCENE 2

(lute music)

Bard: And so the faithful Dolphin traveled to the realm of Atlas, ruler of a distant, mountainous region on earth. There he found Amphritite hiding in a dark cave, far from the wind and waves. At first, she refused to see him (*sound of sobbing*). Only when he shed giant salt tears did she agree to hear what he had to say.

Amphritite: An interesting offer, Dolphin, but I can't imagine living with Poseidon. He's violent, unpredictable, and unreasonable. Look at the way he terrifies innocent sailors. Besides that, he's so ugly! That terrible scowl, and that awful blue hair. . .

Dolphin: Beneath his harsh appearance, my lady, there lies a heart of gold. I beg you to listen to one who knows him well. To all of us who live in his realm, he is a wise and gentle ruler. He would never harm the tiniest crab nor cross the majestic whale. His golden palace is beautiful beyond words. All of this he would share with you.

Amphritite: Why is it then, gentle Dolphin, that he shakes the earth and causes the sea to rage, causing untold agony to so many unfortunate mortals?

Dolphin: Well, he does have a temper, but his anger is only unleashed against those who fail to honor and treat him fairly.

Amphritite: Dolphin, I believe you are honest and intelligent. Do you think. . .

Dolphin: I *know* he is very much in love with you. He mourns because you will not even give him a chance.

Amphritite: This cave *is* getting depressing. Did you say a golden palace?

Dolphin: Just come with me and see, my lady. I'll give you a ride on my back. If you don't like him, you will not be forced to stay.

Amphritite: Promise?

Dolphin: Promise. You have my word.

(lute music)

Bard: And the loyal Dolphin sped back to Poseidon's realm of the sea with the lovely Amphritite on his back. When he saw her, Poseidon had to stop himself from shaking the earth for joy.

With the Dolphin's wise counsel, he persuaded her to become his queen. In time, Amphritite gave birth to a child whose name was Triton. Thereafter, Poseidon was contented to remain in the calm depths of the ocean, occasionally sending Triton to the surface on a golden sea horse to blow up a storm or calm the waves with a mighty blast on his shell.

(conch shell sound)

And with Triton was born an era of peace and prosperity for Greece, in which sailors and land dwellers did not need to fear Poseidon's wrath as long as they remembered to honor him. As for the Dolphin, the sea god did not forget him. Look up at the sky. Poseidon named the constellation "Delphinus" in eternal gratitude, and so that we mortals might be reminded of the creature's intelligence and loyalty.

The constellation Delphinus is located in the Northern hemisphere near Pegasus.

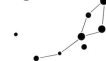

10. Reader's Theater

Work in groups. Act out *Earth Shaker, Wave Maker.* Use instruments or your voices to create the music and sound effects.

11. Write

Pairwork. Imagine your own scene in which one character is angry or afraid of something. Have another character persuade the first character to calm down. Discuss each of these points before you begin to write.

a. The setting. Where and when does the action take place?

b. The characters. Who are they? What are they like?

c. The situation. What does the first character want to persuade the second character to do?

d. The action. What happens?

Write the dialogue for your scene (about 10 lines) and give it a title. Practice reading your scene, then act it out for the whole class.

> **Language Focus**
>
> **Persuasion**
>
> A: I'm not so sure.
> B: Come on, at least give it a try.

1. Preview

Classwork. How are groups of immigrants like ocean waves? How are they different? Look at the graph and discuss these questions.

- What does the graph illustrate?
- What period of American history does it cover?
- What kinds of world events have caused people to immigrate to the United States? Give some examples.
- What kinds of events have slowed down immigration to the United States? Give some examples.

Study Strategy

Making a Time Line

See page 164.

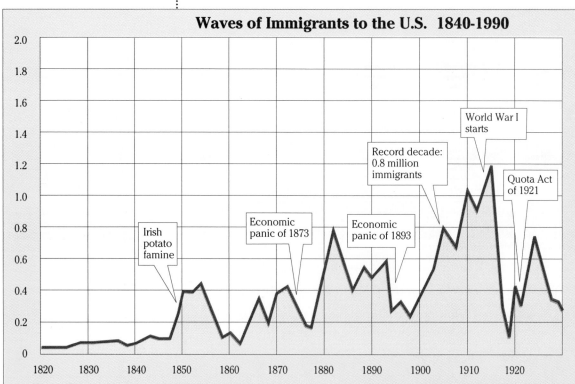

Waves of Immigrants to the U.S. 1840-1990

Irish potato famine

Economic panic of 1873

Economic panic of 1893

Record decade: 0.8 million immigrants

World War I starts

Quota Act of 1921

Recent figures include about 3 million formerly illegal immigrants who received amnesty under 1966 federal law.
Source: U.S. Immigration and Naturalization Service

Pairwork. Work with a partner to match each historical event in the box with its description on the time line. Check the graph to see if you were right. Add other events that have caused large numbers of people to immigrate to the United States.
One item has been done for you.

EVENTS

A. World War II
B. Quota system repealed
C. Great Depression
D. Economic Panic of 1893
E. Amnesty law
F. Irish potato famine
G. Economic panic of 1873
H. Quota act of 1921
I. Vietnam War ends
J. World War I starts

1825

1850
• Potato crop in Ireland fails, causing widespread starvation.

1875
• Period of fear follows over-expansion of business in the U.S.; money loses value, people lose jobs.

• Second period of fear followed by U.S. economic depression.

1900
• U.S. sides with England & France in European war (1914).
• U.S. Congress passes a law restricting immigration (1921).

1925
• Long period of economic slowdown follows stock market crash (1929).
• U.S. joins England, France, & Russia in war against Germany, Italy, & Japan (1944).

_A_

1950
• 1921 law restricting immigration is lifted by U.S. Congress.

• U.S. withdraws from Vietnam; thousands of refugees leave Southeast Asia.

1975

• New law allows many illegal immigrants to apply for permanent residence in the U.S.

2000

Graph (y-axis: 0, 0.2, 0.4, 0.6, 0.8, 1.0, 1.2, 1.4, 1.6, 1.8, 2.0; x-axis: 1930, 1940, 1950, 1960, 1970, 1980, 1990) with labels: Depression, World War II, Quota System repealed, Vietnam war ends, Amnesty law

3. Categorize

Study Strategy:

Classifying

See page 163.

On your own. What kinds of events have caused waves of immigrants to seek better lives in the United States? What factors can cause immigration to slow down? Categorize the events mentioned on the graph into two groups: those that caused immigration to the United States to increase, and those that caused it to decrease.

Increase	Decrease
▪ Irish potato famine	▪ Economic panic of 1873

Study Strategy:

Listening for Specific Information

See page 164.

Classwork. Look at the time line on pages 20–21 again. Imagine what will happen in the future. Suggest some events that might happen after the year 2000. What effects will these events have on the immigration patterns of the 21st century?

4. Listening

You will hear two stories told by immigrants to America. As you listen to each story, take notes on the following information.

A

Date of immigration ⎯⎯⎯⎯⎯⎯⎯⎯⎯⎯⎯

Mode of transportation ⎯⎯⎯⎯⎯⎯⎯⎯⎯⎯

Problems encountered during the trip ⎯⎯⎯⎯

⎯⎯⎯⎯⎯⎯⎯⎯⎯⎯⎯⎯⎯⎯⎯⎯⎯⎯⎯⎯⎯⎯⎯

⎯⎯⎯⎯⎯⎯⎯⎯⎯⎯⎯⎯⎯⎯⎯⎯⎯⎯⎯⎯⎯⎯⎯

 B

Country of origin ————————————————————

Date of immigration ————————————————————

Modes of transportation ————————————————————

Point of entry to the United States ————————————————

Reason for disappointment ————————————————————

————————————————————————————

Plan for the future ————————————————

5. Identify

On your own. Listen to the stories again. Write A, B, or "Both" for each statement.

A. Hendrik Berendregt

B. Saverio Rizzo

_____ came from Europe.

_____ traveled to America by ship.

_____ was already married.

_____ was only 16 years old.

_____ had a difficult voyage.

_____ landed in New York City.

_____ sailed up the Mississippi River.

_____ went to work in a mine.

6. Speculate

Groupwork. Imagine what might have happened to one of the immigrants whose stories you heard. What were their lives like ten years after immigration? What happened to their children and grandchildren? Make a list of possibilities to share with the whole class.

7. Write

a. Groupwork. Think about a move or journey you have made. Why did you leave? How did you travel? What did you hope for? Tell your story to the group. Listen to your classmate's story and ask more questions.

b. On your own. Write a letter about your journey. Decide first who you want to receive your letter. For example, you may want to write to a personal friend, a relative, a teacher, or to the President of the United States. Describe the trip in as much detail as you can remember. For more information on choosing your audience, see page 174.

Shared Reading

Pairwork. The next two pieces were written by young people who were part of more recent waves of immigration. Choose one to read while your partner reads the other one.

A

Could We Ever Forget?

I feel restless.
My thoughts keep going back
To Cambodia,
To when I was born
Into a farmer's life.
How wonderful
Our country was then.

Now I'm far away,
So confused
About my future,
About living in another country
And becoming a citizen.
To go through with it
Would mean good-bye forever.

Ok Kork, 1991

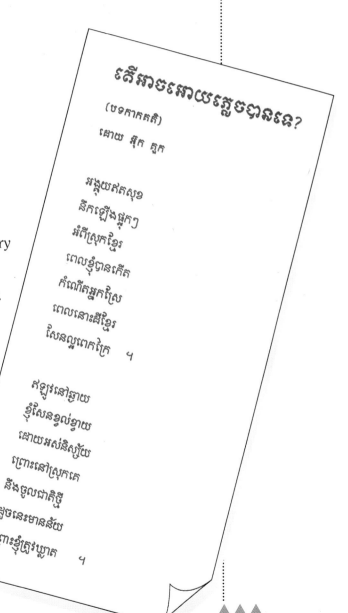

My name is Monique, and I am half-Puerto Rican and half Cuban. It's easy being Puerto Rican because that's what most of my friends are, but it's not easy being Cuban. When I tell people I am half-Cuban, some act dumb and say "so you're a communist." That really gets me mad. Sometimes when I am in classes where the teacher is talking about Cuba, they expect me to know everything just because I am part Cuban. I know a few things about Cuba, but not little details like a specific poem a person made in Cuba during the Spanish-American War or the names of every town and city in Cuba.

One of the best parts of being Cuban is the stories my grandmother tells me about Cuba. Like how, when my dad was about 10 years old, he learned to drive a jeep, and how she had an orange tree in the back of her house, and how she used to go the bakery as a child with her brother to smell the bread and watch how they made it. These little stories make me want to go to Cuba more and more, especially when my grandmother tells me that the water is so blue and clear and the sandy beaches are so pretty. Someday I will go to Cuba, when I am an adult.

Monique Rubio, 1994

9. Compare

Pairwork. Take turns reading Ok Kork's poem and Monique Rubio's personal narrative aloud. Think about how the writers are similar and how they are different.

1. What do these two writers have in common?
   Write two sentences beginning, "They both. . ."

   _____

   _____

2. Now think about the differences. Make notes in a chart like this, then share ideas.

Ok Kork	Monique Rubio

10. Evaluate

Classwork. Which did you like better—the poem or the story? Explain why.

11. Journal Writing

Describe your personal reactions to either the story or the poem. Do you have anything in common with the authors? What questions would you like to ask about their experiences? What would you like to say to them?

Chapter 4: Reflections

*W*hen the wind has died down and there are no waves, it is easier to see your reflection in the water. In periods of calm, people sometimes pause to collect their memories and dreams. In this chapter, you will read three poems that express the beauty of these moments.

1. Visualize

a. On your own. Imagine yourself in a beautiful, peaceful place. You are totally relaxed. Think for five minutes. Make a list of the thoughts that come into your mind.

b. Pairwork. Read your list to a partner. Help each other group your thoughts into three time frames. Make a chart like the one below.

Past	Present	Future

c. Choose the most interesting thing on your partner's chart. Ask your partner to tell you about it in more detail.

2. Preview

On your own. You are going to read an unusual poem. Read about the poet, May Swenson, before you begin. Then look at the whole poem on page 30 at once. What does it look like? In what way is it unusual? Where do you think it begins? Where does it end?

May Swenson (1919-1989)

May Swenson was born into a family of Swedish immigrants who had settled in Logan, Utah. After graduating from Utah State Agricultural College, she worked as a reporter, editor, and teacher. She published eight volumes of poems. She also wrote several short stories and a play, *The Floor*. She died in 1989.

3. Share a Poem

Classwork. Listen to the poem twice and read along.

How Everything Happens

Based on a Study of the Wave by May Swenson

        happen.
        to
        up[1]
     stacking
    is
    something
When nothing is happening

When it happens
    something pulls
       back[2]
       not
        to
         happen.

When   has happened.
   pulling back   stacking up
    happens

   has happened   stacks up.
When it   something   nothing
     pulls back while

Then nothing is happening.
        happens.
       and
      forward
     pushes
    up
   stacks
  something
Then

[1] **stacks up** gets ready
[2] **pulls back** slows down, withdraws

4. Identify

a. Groupwork. Identify the six sentences in the poem. How do you know where each sentence begins and ends? Take turns reading each sentence aloud, moving around the group until you have read the whole poem several times.

b. Pairwork. Copy the diagram of a wave below. Mark places on the diagram where these words and phrases from the poem might fit.

nothing is happening

something is stacking up to happen

it happens

something pulls back

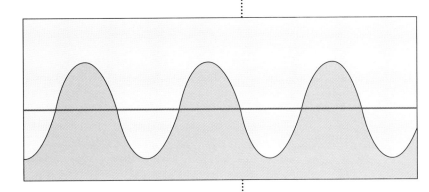

c. Get together with another pair. Compare your diagrams and discuss any differences.

5. Apply

a. Groupwork. Discuss how "something stacks up to happen." What sequence of events lead up to a larger event? Choose one of the examples below or use one of your own.

1. a soccer or football game
2. a party
3. a storm
4. a trip or major move
5. a marriage

b. Use the same example to explain how "something pulls back not to happen."

Example: When one team wins the game, the other team loses.

Language Focus

Time Clauses

When a storm is on the way, people don't plan to have picnics at the beach.

6. Journal Writing

On your own. Imagine yourself back in a beautiful, peaceful place. Reflect on something important that happened in your life. Explain what happened and what led up to it. How did things stack up to happen? Did anything pull back not to happen? How did you feel after it was over?

7. Describe

Pairwork. Discuss this photograph with your partner. Write two sentences that describe the scene.

8. Listen

Listen to the poem several times. Keep looking at the photograph as you listen.

9. Identify

On your own. Who or what is making things happen in the poem? Identify the "doer" of each action. Listen again if you need to.

_____ making footprints and saying words

_____ erasing footprints

_____ carrying away words

10. Read

Pairwork. Take turns reading the whole poem aloud.

AT THE BEACH

by Kemal Ozer

translated by O. Yalim, W. Fielder, and Dionis Riggs

The waves are erasing the footprints
Of those who are walking the beach.

The wind is carrying away the words
Two people are saying to each other.

But still they are walking the beach
Their feet making new footprints.

Still the two are talking together
Finding new words.

Kemal Ozer

Kemal Ozer is a well known modern Turkish poet. He was born in 1935 and lives in Istanbul. "At the Beach" is part of a collection of poems entitled *This Same Sky*. All of the poems in this collection were written in languages other than English.

11. Share Ideas

a. Pairwork. Discuss your reactions to the poem with a partner. Here are some questions to think about.

1. Did you like this poem? Why or why not?

2. What is happening to their footprints and words?

3. Why do they go on making new footprints and saying new words?

4. What other meaning might "footprints" have?

5. What does the poem say about life? Do you agree?

b. Look back at the poem on the first page of this unit. Compare it to "At the Beach." How are the two poems alike? How are they different?

12. Share a Poem

Groupwork. Bring in a poem or song you know. It can be a poem or song written first in another language, then translated into English. Introduce it to your group and read it aloud. If you have a tape of the song or poem, you may want to play it for your group. Answer any questions your classmates may have.

Activity Menu

1. Find the Speed

A wave made with rope has a wavelength of two meters. The frequency of the wave is measured at 0.5 hertz. What is the speed of this wave? When you have an answer, ask a classmate to solve the problem too. Talk about how you found your answers and compare methods.

2. Write a Problem

Write a word problem of your own about waves. Give it to a partner to solve.

3. What's Your Idea?

Draw a picture of water wave patterns near the beach. Explain how you could make measurements of waves like this if you were at the beach. Write your ideas for a classmate.

4. Research an Author's Work

Look up Rachel Carson in an encyclopedia. Write down the titles and publication dates of the books she wrote during her lifetime. Then search in the card or on-line catalogue at your school or local library. Are any of Rachel Carson's books available? If you find a catalogue card or listing for one or more of Rachel Carson's books, write down the call number, the title, and the publication date on a slip of paper or in your notebook. If the book is in the library, find it on the shelves. Ask a librarian if you need help. Report what you found to the class.

5. Identify Ways to Express Emotion

Watch a 30-minute drama on television. Listen for the way the music and sound effects communicate emotions such as happiness, fear, anger, or humor to the television audience. Describe your observations to a partner.

6. Research an Historical Event

Find out more about one of the historical events that has caused immigration to the United States to increase or decrease.

Get the basic facts from an encyclopedia or history textbook:

> What happened?
>
> Where did it happen?
>
> When did it happen?
>
> How did it increase or decrease immigration?

Ask a librarian or teacher if you need help finding information. Take notes on the basic facts, and report back to the class.

7. Debate the Issue

The United States has been called a nation of immigrants, yet today the government has strict rules about immigration. Should the United States allow unlimited immigration? Why or why not? Organize a debate in which one team (Team A) argues for an "open door" immigration policy in which all groups would be allowed to immigrate in unlimited numbers.

The second team (Team B) presents a case for restricting immigration to certain groups or numbers.

Each team gets 15 minutes to prepare a five minute presentation. In the discussion that follows, try to reach a basic principle about immigration upon which all students on both teams can agree.

8. The Power of Waves

Waves can be very destructive. In 1870, a lighthouse was built on the coast of North Carolina. At first, the lighthouse was about 2000 feet from the water. Over the years the waves have eroded[1] the beach. Today the lighthouse stands only 125 feet from the water. Design an advertisement to save this lighthouse. Include answers to these questions: How much closer to the water does the lighthouse get in a year? How many years will it take until the waves reach the lighthouse? What can people do to save the lighthouse?

[1]**eroded**   worn away

Read On

The Education of Berenice Belizaire

by Joe Klein

When Berenice Belizire arrived in New York from Haiti with her mother and sister in 1987, she was not very happy. She spoke no English. The family had to live in a cramped Brooklyn apartment, a far cry from the comfortable house they'd had in Haiti. Her mother, a nurse, worked long hours. School was torture. Berenice had always been a good student, but now she was learning a new language while enduring constant taunts* from the Americans (both black and white). They cursed her in the cafeteria and threw food at her. Someone hit her sister in the head with a book. "Why can't we go home?" Berenice asked her mother.

Because home was too dangerous. The schools weren't always open anymore, and education—her mother insisted—was the most important thing. Her mother had always pushed her: memorize everything, she ordered. "I have a pretty good memory," Berenice admitted last week. Indeed, the other kids at school began to notice that Berenice always, somehow, knew the answers. "They started coming to me for help," she says, "They never called me a nerd."

Within two years Berenice was speaking English, though not well enough to get into one of New York's elite public high schools. She had to settle for the neighborhood school, James Madison—which is one of the magical American places, the alma mater[1] of Ruth Bader Ginsburg[2] among others, a school with a history of unlikely success stories. "I didn't realize what we had in Berenice at first," says math teacher Judith Khan. "She was good at math, but she was quiet. And the things she didn't know! She applied for a summer program in Buffalo[3] and asked me how to get there on the subway. But she always seemed to ask the right questions. She understood the big ideas. She could think on her feet. She could explain difficult problems so the other kids could understand them. Eventually, I realized: she wasn't just pushing for grades, she was hungry for *knowledge*. . . and you know, it never occurred to me that she also was doing it in English and history, all these other subjects that had to be much tougher for her than math."

*taunt   a scornful remark
[1]**alma mater**   the school from which a person graduated
[2]**Ruth Bader Ginsburg**   a justice on the United States Supreme Court

[3]**Buffalo**   a city in New York State, 390 miles northwest from New York City

She moved from third in her class to first during senior year. She was selected as valedictorian,[4] an honor she almost refused (still shy, she wouldn't allow her picture in the school's yearbook). She gave the speech, after some prodding—a modest address about the importance of hard work and how it's never too late to try hard—an immigrant's valedictory.

Last week I caught up with Berenice at the Massachusetts Institute of Technology where she was jump-starting[5] her college career. I asked her what she wanted to be doing in 10 years: "I want to build a famous computer, like IBM," she said. "I want my name to be part of it."

Berenice Belizaire's story is remarkable, but not unusual. The New York City schools are bulging with overachieving immigrants. The burdens[6] they place on a creaky,[7] corroded[8] system are often cited[9] as an argument against liberal[10] immigration policies, but teachers like Judith Khan don't seem to mind. "They're why I love teaching in Brooklyn, " she says. "They have a drive in them we no longer seem to have. You see these kids, who aren't prepared academically and can barely speak the language, struggling so hard. They just sop it up. They're like little sponges. You see Berenice, who had none of the usual, preconceived[11] racial barriers in her mind—you see her becoming friendly with the Russian kids, and learning chess from Po Ching (from Taiwan). It is so exciting.

from Newsweek, Aug. 9, 1993

[4]**valedictorian**	a student, usually with very good grades, who gives the graduation speech
[5]**jump starting**	started early
[6]**burdens**	problems that are difficult to solve.
[7]**creaky**	old and not in good working order
[8]**corroded**	broken down
[9]**cited**	spoken or written about, given as evidence
[10]**liberal**	not strict
[11]**preconceived**	an opinion formed earlier

▲▲▲

Song for Smooth Waters

(Native American, traditional)

Ocean Spirit
calm the waves for me
get close to me, my power
my heart is tired
make the sea like milk for me
yeo
yeholo

West Side

by Naomi Shihab Nye

In certain neighborhoods
the air is paved with names.
Domingo, Monico, Francisco,
shining rivulets of sound.
Names opening wet circles
inside the mouth,
sprinkling bright vowels
across the deserts of
Bill, Bob, John.

The names are worn
on silver linked chains.
Maria lives in Pablo Alley,
Esperanza rides the Santiago bus!
They click together like charms.
O save us from the boarded-up windows,
The pistol crack in a dark backyard,
save us from the leaky roof,
the rattled textbook that never smiles.
Let the names be verses
in a city that sings!

Unit 2:

CHOOSING PATHS

Chapter 1: Making Difficult Decisions

In this chapter, you will think about some of the decisions people make during their lives and read a story about a young woman who has to make a difficult decision.

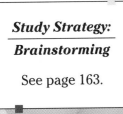

Study Strategy:

Brainstorming

See page 163.

1. Brainstorm

Groupwork. What are some of the important decisions that people make during their lives? List your group's ideas on another piece of paper.

Examples: whether or not to go to college

where to go to college

whether or not to get married

who to marry

Compare ideas with the other groups in your class.

2. Think-Pair-Share

a. On your own. Think of a time when you had to make an important decision. What did you decide to do? Why? How do you feel about your decision today?

b. Pairwork. Get together with a partner. Tell your partner about the decision you made. Listen carefully to your partner's story.

c. Groupwork. Get together with another pair. Tell your partner's story.

Study Strategy:

Previewing

See page 167.

3. Preview

a. Groupwork. Scan the story on pages 44–45. Look for answers to these questions:

1. What's the title of the story?

2. What do you know about the author of this story?

3. Who are the main characters in this story?

4. What do you think this story is about?

Get together with your classmates and compare answers.

Study Strategy:

Making a Tree Diagram

See page 165.

b. Classwork. Read the first four paragraphs of the story. Then share what you know about the main character, Emma Hu. Write your ideas on a tree diagram like this:

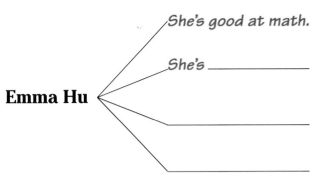

She's good at math.

She's _____

Emma Hu

_____

_____

Share ideas with your classmates and make one tree diagram on the board.

c. On your own. Reread the first four paragraphs. Choose three words that are unfamiliar to you. Try using context to guess the meaning of each word. Then look up each word in the dictionary. Choose the definition that best fits the word in this context. Take notes in a chart like this.

Study Strategy:

Using Context

See page 169.

Example:

New words	My guess from context	Dictionary definition
nasty	unfriendly	unpleasant in manner; angry

Tell your classmates about the words in your chart.

 **4. Read**

On your own. As you read the first part of the story on pages 44–45, write your thoughts and questions in your journal. Also, try using context to guess the meaning of any unfamiliar words.

Who's Hu? (Part 1)

by Lensey Namioka

I was tired of being a freak.[1]

My father was a professor of mathematics at M.I.T., and whenever I got 100 on my math test (which was pretty often) my high school teachers would say, "I know where Emma Hu gets help with her homework . . . cackle[2] . . . cackle . . ." The rest of the class usually cackled along. At first I didn't see why they were so nasty about it. Later I discovered that girls in this country weren't supposed to be good in math. The teachers didn't like it when Arthur Aldrich—our self-styled math genius—corrected their mistakes in class. They hated it a lot more when I did.

In China there was nothing wrong with girls being good at math. In fact, Chinese women were supposed to keep the household or business accounts. But in America, when I opened my big mouth to correct my algebra teacher—in broken English, yet—everyone thought I was a freak. Once I thought I would cheat on my math test by deliberately making a couple of mistakes, but when it came to the point, I just couldn't do it. Mathematics was too beautiful to mess up.

On most days I wasn't too bothered by my math grades, but lately I had begun to worry. I was a senior at Evesham High, a high school in the suburbs of Boston, and the senior prom[3] was only three weeks away. Who was going to ask a Chinese girl math whiz?[4] According to my friend Katey, everybody went to the prom except freaks.

After lunch the first class I attended was math. Just being in the classroom made me feel better. I liked to look around the room at the portion of the blackboard painted with a permanent white grid for graphing equations, the hanging cardboard models of regular polyhedra we had made as a class project, and the oak shelf containing plaster models of conic sections and various surfaces. My favorite was the hyperbolic paraboloid, or saddle, with its straight lines neatly incised in the plaster.

The class was Advanced Mathematics, intended for seniors who were going into science or math and who had already taken algebra, geometry, and trig. The course covered analytic geometry, calculus, and a little probability theory. Actually, it wasn't so much the content of the course that I liked best: it was the teacher, Mr. Antonelli. He was a short man only a little taller than I, and he had a swarthy face dominated by a huge beak of a nose. Unlike my other math teachers (one of them even a woman), he didn't seem to find it bizarre that a girl should do well in his class. As for my being Chinese, I doubt if he even noticed. Mr. Antonelli didn't care if you were a Martian robot, as long as you did the math correctly.

Today Mr. Antonelli gave the impression of suppressed excitement. He clearly had something on his mind,[5] because for the first time I remember, he let one of the boys do a maximum-minimum problem without checking the second derivative to see if it was an inflection point. Arthur Aldrich and I

[1]freak	a strange or weird person
[2]cackle	shrill laughter
[3]senior prom	dance party for seniors before they graduate
[4]whiz	genius, very smart person
[5]had something on his mind	was thinking about something

▲▲▲

beat each other to a draw[6] in pointing out the mistake. Mr. Antonelli acknowledged our reproof[7] almost absentmindedly. He certainly was preoccupied.[8]

With five minutes left of the period, Mr. Antonelli made an announcement: "Class, you remember that last fall you all took the semi-final exam for the Sterns Mathematics Prize. Today I received word of the results."

The Sterns was a mathematics prize given annually to a high school senior in Massachusetts. The award was for $200, but the prestige it carried was immeasurable. Never in the history of the Sterns Prize had it been won by a girl.

"Now," Mr. Antonelli went on, "it is an honor for our school if a student here makes it to the finals. Well, we've got not just one student, but two who are going into the finals. One is Arthur Aldrich."

Arthur was a tall, gangly[9] boy with hair so blond that it looked almost white. With his long nose and sharp chin, he reminded me of a white fox in one of the Chinese fairy tales. Arthur had very few stumbling blocks[10] in his life. His family was comfortably off,[11] he did well in every subject in school, and he was a credit to the Evasham High School track team. In spite of his successes, Arthur was too arrogant[12] to be popular.

"The other," Mr. Antonelli announced, "is Emma Hu."

The class cheered. My thoughts were in a whirl. I thought I had fallen down badly[13] on the exam the previous fall because there were two problems I hadn't been able to do. Now it seemed that my performance hadn't been so bad after all.

I have only the vaguest memories of my other classes that afternoon. I barely realized when the final bell rang. Leaving school, I almost hugged my books to my chest. It was like waking up on my birthday and finding a pile of presents outside my door.

I was so absorbed that I didn't hear footsteps coming up behind me. I jumped when Arthur's voice spoke in my ear. "I want to talk to you."

"About what?" I asked, surprised. In Arthur's ranking of animal intelligence, girls came somewhere between sheep and myna birds. Of course that made me even more of a freak in his eyes.

Arthur grinned now. In the illustrations of my Chinese fairy tale book, foxes grinned with their mouths forming a big V. Arthur's smile was just like that. "I hear you want to go to the senior prom but can't find anyone to take you. I have a simple proposition to make: I'll take you to the prom—refreshments, corsage,[14] dinner afterward, the whole works—if you'll drop out of[15] the Sterns exam."

[6] beat each other to a draw	tied, were even
[7] reproof	criticism
[8] preoccupied	worried
[9] gangly	tall, thin, and ungraceful
[10] stumbling blocks	barriers, difficulties
[11] comfortably off	without financial problems
[12] arrogant	proud
[13] fallen down badly	not done well
[14] corsage	flowers to pin on one's dress
[15] drop out of	leave; decide not to participate in

5. Distinguishing Fact and Opinion

Groupwork. Share ideas about these characters from the story. Add information to a chart like this.

Emma Hu	Mr. Antonelli	Arthur Aldrich
Her father teaches math. (F)	*He's a good teacher. (O)*	*He's tall. (F)*

Language Focus:

Expressing Possible Consequences

- If Emma accepts Arthur's proposition, Mr. Antonelli will be disappointed.
- If she accepts Arthur's proposition, she won't _____.
- If she rejects his proposition, she will probably feel _____.

Look back over the information on your chart. Put an (F) next to the facts. Put an (O) next to any opinions. Then compare charts with the other groups in your class.

6. Speculate

Classwork. In the story, Arthur makes a proposition.

I have a simple proposition to make: I'll take you to the prom if you drop out of the Sterns exam.

If Emma accepts Arthur's proposition, what will the consequences be? If she rejects his proposition, what will happen? List your ideas on the board.

If she accepts his proposition,. . .

_____

_____

_____

If she rejects his proposition,. . .

_____

_____

_____

Study Strategy:

Predicting

See page 167.

7. Predict

a. Pairwork. How do you think Emma will respond to Arthur's proposition? Write your prediction.

b. Pairwork. Role play the conversation between Emma and Arthur on page 45. Add your own ideas to continue their conversation.

8. Read

On your own. Read the rest of the story to check your prediction from Activity 7.

Who's Hu? (Part 2)

The sheer gall[1] of Arthur's proposition took my breath away, and for a moment I was too astounded even to be angry. In the end my main reaction turned out to be triumph. "So you're really afraid I might do better than you on the exam!" I said, unable to hide my satisfaction.

Two spots of color appeared on Arthur's pale cheeks, but he kept his foxy grin. "I can do better than you any day, don't you worry! But I know you're desperate to go to the prom. Every red-blooded, normal high school senior goes to the prom, right?"

I said nothing. The price of being a red-blooded, normal high school senior was pretty high.

"Well?" demanded Arthur.

I was determined to be equally curt. "No," I said.

He stormed away[2] without another word.

"I'm terribly sorry. I couldn't help overhearing."

I turned around and saw it was Kim. He was a Korean boy who was one of my mother's music students.

It was almost a relief not to have to pretend. "It doesn't matter," I said. To my fury, my lips were beginning to quiver.[3] "There isn't a person in school who doesn't already know I haven't been able to find a date for the prom. It's been a joke for so long that I don't even feel humiliated about it anymore."

But that was a lie.

Kim looked as if he were trying not to laugh. "I don't even try to understand all these American customs anymore. But this prom sounds like some sort of native ritual or tribal dance."

He was a foreigner in America and not bothered by it at all. He was even inviting me to join him in enjoying the amusing antics[4] of the natives.

"Don't you feel lonely sometimes?" I asked, remembering my loneliness the first day of school on discovering I was to be the only Chinese there. That loneliness I suffered until Katey and her friends took me in.[5]

[1]**gall**	nerve; rudeness
[2]**stormed away**	left angrily
[3]**quiver**	tremble; shake
[4]**antics**	strange behavior
[5]**took me in**	accepted me; made me part of their group

Kim only smiled and shook his head. "I'm too busy. Schoolwork is hard for me because of my poor English, and after school all my time is taken up with practicing. Even if I had the money, I wouldn't go." He looked at me curiously. "You are devoted to mathematics the way I am to music, aren't you? I think I heard your mother say so."

I nodded, grateful for these words. He considered our situations to be comparable, and he didn't think that a girl being interested in math was any stranger than a boy being interested in music.

As Kim got on his bus, he said, "You should try to do the best you can on the exam. You owe it to yourself."

• • •

On the appointed afternoon, I entered the Boston University classroom where the Sterns examination was being held. The monitor checked my name against his list and nodded. "Good. All fifty of you are now here."

It seemed I was the last one to arrive. For a while I had considered not coming at all.

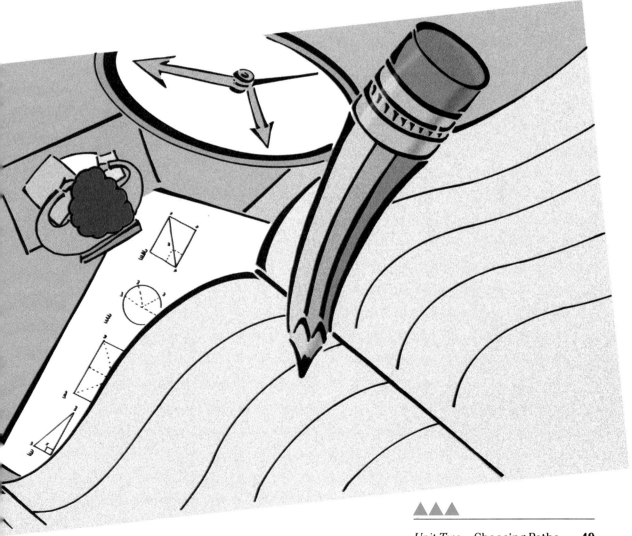

What was the point? I was in no condition to do mathematics. I suppose I came because it would have been too much trouble to tell Mr. Antonelli I was planning to drop out.

We all sat down and arranged our pencils and bluebooks[6] on the desks in front of us. When the monitor passed out the exams, heads bent eagerly over the papers. I looked at the first page with dull despair. There were some diagrams with circles, but nothing made sense to me. In my present state I hardly knew the difference between an ellipse and a circle. An ellipse was just a tired circle.

All around me pencils scratched busily in bluebooks. On my left, Arthur glanced up at me. He looked different, and I realized he had applied a pomade on his hair to stick it down. He flashed his foxy grin, and the smugness in

it told me I looked a mess. I had not slept at all the night before, and my eyes were red and puffy—not all from sleeplessness.

My watch showed that almost an hour had passed. Already half the time allotted for the exam was gone and I hadn't started a single problem.

I glanced at Arthur again and found his eyes fastened on me eagerly. How many times had he looked this way? He must have noticed that I hadn't done a thing, because when his eyes met mine, his grin widened triumphantly.

I picked up the exam paper and looked at it once more. The writing might as well have been in Greek. Only I could read Greek a little, since I already knew all the Greek letters from seeing them used in mathematics. No, the writing here might as well be in Korean for all I could understand.

Kim entered my mind. He could not afford to give up classical music, for he owed it to himself not to squander[7] his talent.

It was the thought of Kim that finally opened my eyes. I should not try to be something I was not. And I was not, nor could ever be, a normal American teenager. I was going to be a mathematician. This was the Sterns exam, my first opportunity to show my mettle.[8] I could not afford to squander my talent. As Kim had said, I owed it to myself. I had to stop frittering[9] away the precious minutes and get down to work. Having made the decision, I felt a weight lift from my chest.

[6]**bluebooks**   booklets in which students write examination answers
[7]**squander**   waste; use foolishly
[8]**mettle**   courage
[9]**frittering**   wasting

About the Author

Lensey Namioka is a Chinese American writer who is known for her historical and fantasy stories. The story "Who's Hu?" is an excerpt from a novel of the same name.

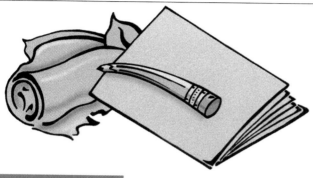

9. **Share Ideas**

Language Focus:

Asking for and Stating Opinions

We think that going to the prom was important to Emma because her friends were going and she didn't want to be left out.

a. Groupwork. Write three opinion-questions based on the story *Who's Hu?* (Opinion-questions do not have a right or wrong answer.)

Examples: Why do you think going to the senior prom was important to Emma?

b. Write your group's questions on the board. Look over the other groups' questions on the board and choose one question to discuss in your group. Let one person record your group's ideas.

c. Tell the class which question your group chose. Report any differences of opinion among the members of your group and identify any conclusions your group reached.

d. Choose another question from the list on the board and repeat the process.

10. Make a Story Map

Study Stategy:

Making a Story Map

See page 164.

a. Pairwork. What happened in the story *Who's Hu?* Organize your ideas on a story map like this:

b. Get together with another pair. Use your story map to retell the story *Who's Hu?* Take turns giving information.

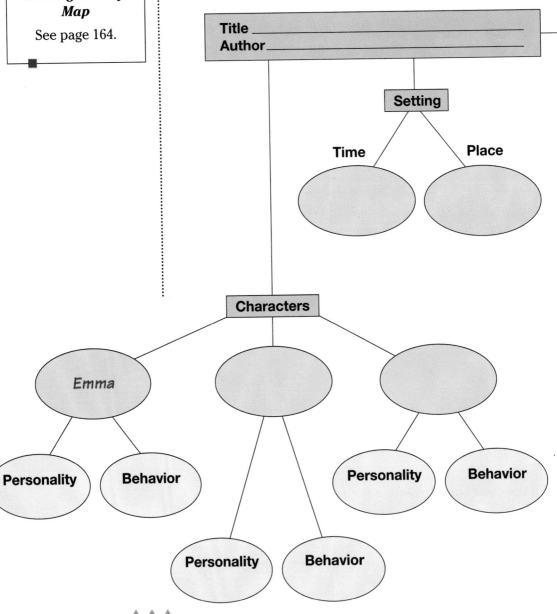

Title _____

Author _____

Setting

Time   Place

Characters

Emma

Personality   Behavior

Personality   Behavior

Personality   Behavior

11. Reflect

On your own. What choices does Emma make in the story? Do you think she makes good choices? Why or why not? How would you have acted in this situation? Why? Write your response in your journal.

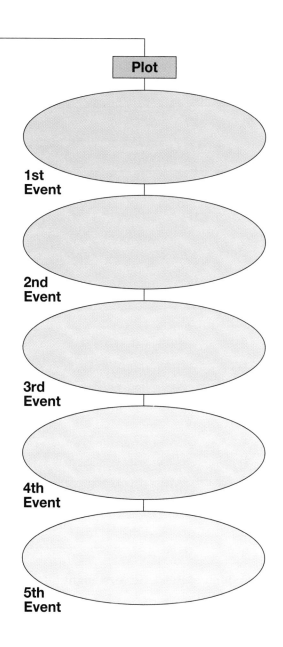

Plot

1st Event

2nd Event

3rd Event

4th Event

5th Event

Chapter 2: Career Paths

*W*hat career path do you think you will follow? What choices will you probably make along the way? In this chapter you will look at the career path of a well-known writer and then research the career path of another person.

1. List

a. Classwork. Study the chart below. Then think of different careers in each area of work. Add your ideas to a chart on the board.

Work Areas	Careers	
Health	Doctor Hospital Administrator Nurse Physical Therapist	Dietician Pharmacist
Education		
Arts		
Science/Technology		
Sports		
Business		
Travel		

b. Pairwork. Which of these careers might interest you? Why? Tell a partner.

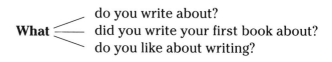

2. ▷ Preview

Groupwork. In the reading on page 57, Nicholasa Mohr tells about the path she followed to become a writer. Imagine that you are going to interview Ms. Mohr. What questions would you ask? List your group's questions on another piece of paper.

What ⟨ do you write about?
did you write your first book about?
do you like about writing?

When ⟨

Why ⟨

Where ⟨

Who ⟨

Write your group's questions on the board.
Look over the other groups' questions.

3. ▷ Read

On your own. Read pages 57–58 to look for answers to your questions from Activity 2.

Nicholasa Mohr

From the moment my mother handed me some scrap paper, a pencil, and a few crayons, I decided that by making pictures and writing letters I could create my own world, like "magic." In the small, crowded apartment I shared with my large family (six older brothers, parents, aunt, and a boy cousin), "making magic" permitted me all the space and freedom my imagination could handle.

I was born in the urban village in the heart of New York City's Manhattan known as "El Barrio," meaning "the neighborhood." Also known as Spanish Harlem, it is the oldest Spanish-speaking community in the city. My parents had migrated with four small children from the island of Puerto Rico before the Second World War. Like many other strangers preceding them, they hoped that with hard work and opportunity they too could offer their children that good life known as the American Dream. Subsequently three more children were born, of which I was the youngest and only daughter.

We moved to the Bronx, where I spent most of my formative[1] years. Through the loss of my parents and separation from my family in my early teens, I continued to rely on my ability to draw and to tell stories. After high school, I enrolled in the Art Students League and pursued my career as a fine artist. I studied in the Taller de Graficos in Mexico City, returned, and continued to study at the Brooklyn Museum Art School, the New School for Social Research, and the Pratt Center for Printmaking. I got married and had two sons, David and Jason. All of this time I worked and exhibited my prints and paintings in New York City galleries. In 1972 when I was asked to do a book jacket for Harper and Row[2] I showed them fifty pages of vignettes[3] I had written dealing with my childhood. The result was a contract and my first book. *Nilda* was published in 1973. I also did the book jacket and eight illustrations for *Nilda*.

What I thought would have been a temporary diversion[4] (I assumed I'd return to visual art and be done with this business of writing!) turned out to be my new focus[5] in life. Writing satisfied and fulfilled my needs to communicate in a way I had not

---

[1]**formative years**   years in which a person develops
[2]**Harper and Row** a publishing company in New York
[3]**vignettes**   short written descriptions
[4]**diversion**   turning point
[5]**focus**   centering activity

experienced as a visual artist. *Nilda* is the most autobiographical of my books, not so much in fact (it takes place during the Second World War) but in feeling and circumstances. This was followed by *El Bronx Remembered*, a collection of short stories and a novella dealing with the decade of the promised future for Puerto Rican immigrants, 1946-1956. My next book was *In Nueva York*, a collection of interrelated stories about the Hispanic community in New York City's Lower East Side, during the end of the Vietnam War. *Felita*, a novel for younger children, is about contemporary times. It shows how a family is forced out of an all-white neighborhood and back to their barrio, and how in spite of this setback and humiliation, they pull together and continue to build a future for themselves. *Rituals of Survival*, an adult book, is a collection of stories about the struggles and courage of Puerto Rican women. This was followed by *Going Home*, a sequel to *Felita*. In this novel, Felita visits Puerto Rico to discover that she is seen as an outsider, a gringa, and she must deal with her identity. I have recently completed two plays and an original fairy tale. In celebration of my work, the State University of New York at Albany has awarded me an honorary Doctor of Letters degree.

Growing up, I had never seen or read any book that included Puerto Ricans (or Hispanics, for that matter) as citizens who worked hard and contributed to this nation. In American letters,[6] we were *invisible*. Writing has given me the opportunity to establish my own sense of history and existence as a Puerto Rican woman in the literature of these United States. I know that even if I had been born rich, and white Anglo-Saxon Protestant, I would still be doing creative work . . . i.e., visual art and writing. However, because of who I am, I feel blessed by the work I do, for it permits me to use my imagination and continue to "make magic." With this magic, I can recreate those deepest of personal memories as well as validate[7] and celebrate my heritage and my future.

[6]**letters**   literature
[7]**validate**   confirm; see as worthwhile and acceptable

4. Share Information

a. Pairwork. Share any answers you found to your questions from Activity 2.

b. What do you learn about Nicholasa Mohr from her autobiographical account? Add information to each category in a chart like this:

painting

```
┌─────────────────┐                                    ┌─────────────────┐
│    Childhood     │                                    │    Interests     │
└─────────────────┘                                    └─────────────────┘
              \                                        /
               \          ╭───────────────────╮      /
                \         │  Nicholasa Mohr    │     /
                /         ╰───────────────────╯      \
               /                                      \
┌─────────────────┐                                    ┌─────────────────┐
│    Education     │                                    │ Accomplishments  │
└─────────────────┘                                    └─────────────────┘
```

Get together with another pair and share information.

c. Identify important events in Mohr's career path. Collect information in a diagram like this:

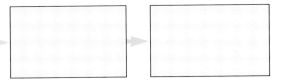

Get together with another pair. Use your diagram to tell about Mohr's career path. Take turns giving information.

d. On your own. Use your diagram to write a one-paragraph summary of Mohr's career path. Include only the most important information in your summary.

> **Language Focus:**
> **Using Time Words**
>
> When she was a child, she liked to draw.
> While she was in high school, ____.
> After high school, she ____.
> Following high school, ____.

5. Listen

a. Classwork. The photographs below give information about Luis Herrera. What can you guess about his career path from these pictures? Share ideas with your classmates.

b. On your own. The report you are going to hear was written by Jaime Chavez, a student at Jersey City State College. In his report, Chavez tells about the career path of Luis Herrera. As you listen to the report, take notes in a chart like this:

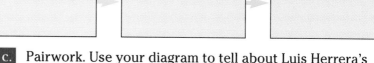

c. Pairwork. Use your diagram to tell about Luis Herrera's career path. Take turns giving information.

6. Investigate

Find out about the career path of someone who interests you. This might be a well-known person or someone you know personally. In writing, tell your classmates about the important events in this person's career. Here are some suggestions to help you get started:

a. With a group of classmates, make a list of people you might want to research. Look through textbooks and library books for possible subjects.

b. Think of people you know personally. What career paths have they followed? List the name of anyone you might want to write about.

c. Choose one person to find out about. Be sure to choose someone who really interests you. If you want to write about someone you know personally, make sure you have a good source of information (someone to get information from).

d. What do you want to find out about this person's career path? Make a list of questions. Write your questions in a chart like this:

Person's Name: _____		
Questions	Answers	Sources (where you found the answers)

e. Look in the library for several sources of information. Read about the person you chose and take notes in your chart. Be sure to write down your source of information. If you are collecting information about someone you know personally, interview that person and take notes.

f. Tell a classmate about this person's career path. Answer any questions your classmate has. If you need to do more research, go back to the library.

g. Look back over your notes and circle the information you want to include in your writing.

h. Write a first draft of your paper.

i. Refer to the Writer's Guide on pages 174–175 for suggestions on how to revise your first draft.

Chapter 3: The Underground Railroad

The Underground Railroad was a secret network of people who helped runaway slaves escape to freedom. In this chapter, you will find out how the Underground Railroad worked and read a play about a group of people who used the Undergound Railroad to escape from slavery.

1. Preview

Classwork. Read the questions below. Then look over the pictures on pages 63–65 and read the first two paragraphs of the passage. On another piece of paper, write any answers you find.

Questions	Answers
1. What was the Underground Railroad?	
2. Who used the Underground Railroad?	
3. When did the Underground Railroad exist?	
4. How did the Underground Railroad help people to escape?	

2. Read

On your own. As you read pages 63–65, look for answers to the questions in Activity 1.

The Underground Railroad

The Underground Railroad wasn't underground and it wasn't a railroad. But it was real just the same. And it was one of the brightest chapters in American history.

The Underground Railroad was a secret network of people who helped slaves flee[1] to freedom before the Civil War (1861–65). The slaves were black people from families who had been brought from Africa in chains. They were owned by their white masters and forced to work without pay.

The first slaves arrived in Jamestown, Virginia in 1619. Two hundred years later, there were nearly four million slaves in the United States. Most worked on large plantations in the South. By then, slavery had been outlawed[2] in most northern states.

Many slaves were treated cruelly. Some were not. All could be bought and sold. Some slaves bought their own freedom by earning money during time off from work at the plantation. There were free black people in both the North and South during slavery days.

Thousands of slaves ran away each year. Some fled to get away from harsh masters. Others wanted to enjoy liberty. The Underground Railroad was started to help them.

The "stations" of the Underground Railroad were homes, shops, and churches where runaway slaves were hidden and fed. The "agents" or "stationmasters" were people—both black and white—who hated slavery. They wanted to help slaves get free.

"Conductors" on the Underground Railroad led or transported fugitives[3] from station to station on their way to free states. They had to watch for slave catchers, who were paid to capture runaways and return them. Some conductors guided slaves all the way to Canada.

[1]**flee**   run away
[2]**outlawed**   declared against the law
[3]**fugitives**   people who are running away from something

The most famous conductor was Harriet Tubman. She was a strong, determined woman. Before she became a conductor, Mrs. Tubman had been a passenger on a dangerous journey on the Underground Railroad.

She lived as a slave on a plantation in Maryland. One day in 1849, Mrs. Tubman heard that she was going to be sold. She decided to escape instead.

Harriet Tubman walked away from the plantation that night. She followed the North Star toward the free state of Pennsylvania 90 miles away. Sometimes she hiked all night, from station to station on the Underground Railroad. Once she was hidden under blankets and vegetables in a farm wagon, and she rode through the night. Another time she was carried in a rowboat for miles.

She got to Pennsylvania one morning just at sunrise. Years later she recalled that moment:

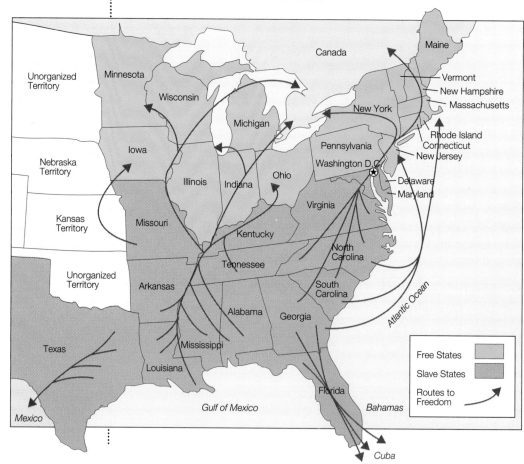

"I looked at my hands to see if I was the same person now I was free. There was such a glory over everything, the sun came like gold through the trees and over the fields, and I felt like I was in heaven."

Soon Harriet Tubman became a conductor on the Underground Railroad. Over the next 10 years, she made 19 trips into the slave states and guided 300 slaves to freedom.

We can only guess how many slaves used the Underground Railroad. Historians estimate the total at between 40,000 and 100,000 by the time the Civil War began in 1861. The war was fought in large part over the slavery issue.

In 1863, President Abrahm Lincoln declared slaves free. That was the end of the Underground Railroad. There were no ceremonies and no celebrations. The invisible railroad ended as it began—quietly and without fanfare.[4]

Robert W. Peterson

[4]**fanfare**   noisy celebration

Study Strategy:
Using Context
See page 169.

3. **Define**

Pairwork. In the reading on pages 63–65, the terms listed below have a special meaning. Look back over the reading to help you define these words as they relate to the Underground Railroad.

Terms	Railroad	Underground Railroad
station	place where trains stop to pick up and drop off passengers	
stationmaster	person who runs the train station	
conductor	person who takes care of passengers on the train	
passenger	person who rides in a train	

Why do you think people used these words when they talked about the Underground Railroad? Share ideas with your classmates.

4. **Share Ideas**

Groupwork. Share ideas about the passage. Here are some questions you can discuss in your group:

a. What interested you about the Underground Railroad? Why?

b. What else would you like to find out about the Underground Railroad? Where could you find the answers to your questions?

c. What choices did Harriet Tubman make? What risks did she take?

d. Why do you think some people chose to become conductors on the Underground Railroad? What risks did they take?

a. Classwork. The following play is about a group of fugitives on the Underground Railroad. Look over the play quickly. What do you know about the characters in the play?

b. Imagine that you are one of the characters in this play. As you read the play, think about the choices this person makes. After you finish reading the play, share ideas with your classmate.

The Douglass "Station" of the Underground Railroad

by Glennette Tilley Turner

Cast: *Frederick Douglass   First Son   Harriet Tubman   First Narrator*
Anna Douglass   Second son   Eight Fugitive Slaves   Second Narrator

First Narrator:	It is late one night in early November, sometime after the 1850 Fugitive Slave Act[1] has become law. Harriet Tubman and a party of eight fugitive slaves have just arrived outside the Douglass home in Rochester, New York.
Second Narrator:	Harriet Tubman goes from a wooded area to the back door, trying to stay in the shadows of the house. Her knock is so quiet it can hardly be heard.
Harriet:	(*Knock, knock. Pause. Knock, knock.*)
First Narrator:	One of Douglass' sons looks out the window and whispers:
First son:	It's Moses.
Second Narrator:	Frederick Douglass turns the lamplight off and goes to the door—just barely opening it.

[1]**Fugitive Slave Act**   law requiring that slaves who had escaped to states where slavery was outlawed be captured and returned to their owners.

Frederick Douglass:	Come in, Moses.
First narrator:	Harriet Tubman steps inside, and whispers . . .
Harriet Tubman:	I have eight. I had them wait in the woods 'til I knew it was safe to come in.
Frederick Douglass:	One of my sons is the lookout.[2] He let us know you were nearby and that the coast is clear.[3]
Anna Douglass:	Welcome, Harriet. Have them come in.
Second Narrator:	Harriet Tubman signals to her company of slaves. One at a time they approach the house just as she had done.
First Narrator:	Douglass barely opens the door and admits the slaves. Once they are inside, they gather near the fireplace to warm themselves after their long journey. Some are barefooted; others are wearing summer-weight clothes.
Frederick Douglass:	Congratulations. Moses has brought you to the doorstep of freedom. The land of Canada is just across the lake. You'll be there by this time tomorrow night.
Anna Douglass:	Meanwhile, here's food and some blankets so you can eat and then rest.
First Narrator:	She gestures to an iron pot in the fireplace and blankets in the corner.
Frederick Douglass:	I know from experience what it's like to escape. You really can't relax until you get to the Promised Land.
Second Narrator:	The Douglass' second son appears at the door with a huge ladle and dishes up stew for everyone. In the meantime the first son has gone to take his turn as the lookout.
Anna Douglass to Harriet Tubman:	How was your trip?
Harriet Tubman:	(*eating like she's really hungry, but in a hurry to get through—talks between mouthfuls*) We had lots of close calls, but made it safely this far. Main thing was trying to race the snow. Didn't want that to catch us. Can't take the chance of leaving tracks.[4]
Frederick Douglass to Harriet Tubman:	Which route did you take this time?

[2] **lookout**	person who keeps watch
[3] **the coast is clear**	no enemies are nearby
[4] **tracks**	footprints; marks

Harriet Tubman:	(*obviously worried about something as she talks*) Eastern Shore to Wilmington in Delaware. Some of the young ones got scared when they heard the slave catchers' dogs. We had to wade in water so the dogs would lose our scent.
Frederick Douglass:	It must have been a relief to reach Thomas Garrett's house in Wilmington, wasn't it?
Harriet Tubman:	(*trying to answer Douglass' question, although it is more and more obvious she has something else on her mind*) Yes, he gave us dry clothes and we slept a while. He had a former friend take us to Philadelphia in a wagon with a false bottom.
Frederick Douglass:	Where William Still met you—right?
Harriet Tubman:	Yes. (*then, putting her dish down abruptly*) Excuse me, Frederick, but what's the plan for us going from here to Canada?
Frederick Douglass:	I've arranged for a friend to get you and your party on the morning train. You'll have to board before daylight, so you won't be seen. Hope you don't mind having to travel in the baggage car. It's getting harder and harder to cross the border.
Harriet Tubman:	Let me stop you, Frederick. I thank you for what you're planning, but I won't feel safe 'til we get on the Canadian side. Can you possibly get somebody to take us across the lake tonight? All of a sudden I had this strange feeling the slave catchers are on our trail.
Anna Douglass:	Can't you wait until morning? As tired as you all are, a good night's sleep would do you some good.
Harriet Tubman:	Thank you, Anna. I am bone tired and the others are too, but I can't chance waiting. Morning may be too late.
Frederick Douglass:	What makes you so sure slave catchers are trailing you?
Harriet Tubman:	There's a $40,000 reward on my head and lots of people want to cash in. I don't know what gave me this feeling, but my hunches[5] have been right too many times before to ignore them.
First Narrator:	Douglass' second son has made an inconspicuous exit while his parents talked with Harriet Tubman. That son now reappears and announces,
Second Son:	Excuse me for interrupting, but my brother and I have arranged to take you across the lake.

[5]**hunches**   suspicions; feelings

▲▲▲

Harriet Tubman:	Oh, thank you. (*turning to Frederick and Anna*) You certainly raised your sons well. Thank you all!
Second Narrator:	Harriet gathers her things and wakens the fugitives in her group.
Harriet Tubman:	Hurry now. It's time to go.
Frederick Douglass:	(*shaking Harriet's hand*) Have a safe journey, Moses.
Anna Douglass:	(*giving Harriet a hug*) God be with you.
First Son:	(*in an urgent whisper*) The coast is clear. Let's go.
First Narrator:	Harriet and the fugitives walk in the shadows as the Douglass' first son leads the way to the shores of Lake Ontario.
Second Narrator:	There the second son is waiting to help them into a boat and they all set out for the Canadian shore.

6. Role Play

Work in groups of eight. Follow the suggestions below to act out *The Douglass Station of the Underground Railroad.*

a. Assign a role to each person in your group.

b. Think about the setting of the play. Where are the characters when the play begins? Where is the door of the Douglass house? What is inside the house?

c. Practice reading the play. Consider what your character is thinking and feeling as you read the lines. Use appropriate body language when you speak.

d. Change roles and read the play again.

e. Perform your version of the play for your classmates or for another class.

7. Trace a Route

Groupwork. In the play, Harriet Tubman mentions three places that she and the eight fugitives travel through. Find these places on a U.S. map. Then answer the questions below:

a. How did they get to Wilmington, Delaware? What problems did they have along the way?

b. How did they get from Wilmington to Philadelphia? How long do you think it took?

c. How did they get from Rochester to Canada? How long do you think it took?

8. Write

a. On your own. Imagine that you are a stationmaster, a conductor, or a fugitive on the Underground Railroad. Write a diary entry telling about a day on the Railroad. You can use the questions below to help you get started.

- What happened on this day?

- What difficulties did you encounter?

- What choices did you make?

b. Get together with several classmates. Take turns reading your diary entries aloud.

Chapter 4: Choosing a Path

*W*hat path will you take in the future? What choices will you make? In this chapter, you will find out how two poets answer these questions.

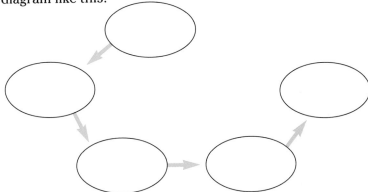

1. Predict

a. On your own. What path will you take in the future? Think of some of the things you hope to do. Write your ideas on a diagram like this:

b. Tell a partner about the things on your path.

Language Focus:

Future Plans and Possiblities

- I hope to go to college.
- I plan to ___.
- I intend to ___.

2. Shared Reading

a. On your own. Read the poem on page 73 several times. Keep these thoughts in mind as you read.

- A poem can mean different things to different people.
- There is no one correct interpretation of a poem.
- Each time you read a poem, you may see and hear different things.

b. Groupwork. Choose one stanza from the poem. Together, practice reading your group's stanza aloud. Then read your stanza aloud to the class.

THE ROAD NOT TAKEN

Two roads diverged[1] in a yellow wood,
And sorry I could not travel both
And be one traveler, long I stood
And looked down one as far as I could
To where it bent in the undergrowth;[2]

Then took the other, as just as fair,[3]
And having perhaps the better claim,
Because it was grassy and wanted wear;[4]
Though as for that the passing there
Had worn them really about the same,

And both that morning equally lay
In leaves no step had trodden black.
Oh, I kept the first for another day!
Yet knowing how way leads on to way,
I doubted if I should ever come back.

I shall be telling this with a sigh
Somewhere ages and ages hence:[5]
Two roads diverged in a wood, and I—
I took the one less traveled by,
And that has made all the difference.

Robert Frost

About the Author

Robert Frost is one of America's favorite poets. He was born in 1874 in San Francisco, but lived much of his life in New England. Many of his poems have New England settings. Frost read one of his poems at the inauguration of President John F. Kennedy in 1961. He died in 1963.

[1]**diverged**   went in different directions
[2]**undergrowth**   plants growing around trees
[3]**fair**   beautiful
[4]**wanted wear**   had not been used much
[5]**hence**   after now; in the future

3. Share Ideas

Groupwork. Get together with your classmates and share ideas about the poem. Choose one or more of these questions to discuss in your group.

a. What do you see as you read the poem?

b. How would you describe the narrator of this poem? What do you know about this person?

c. Describe the two roads in the poem. How are they different

d. How might you connect the poem to your life?

Language Focus:

Expressing Regrets

- I wish I had spent less time working.
- I wish I hadn't gotten married so young.

---

4. Write

On your own. In the last stanza of the poem, the poet says "I shall be telling this with a sigh/Somewhere ages and ages hence." Imagine that you are 80 years old. Describe the road you took in life. Are you happy with this road? Why or why not? What do you wish you had done differently?

---

5. Preview

a. Classwork. Do you ever choose the easiest way to do something, even if it is not the best way? This is sometimes called "taking the easy way out." Look at the choices below and identify "the easy way out."

	or	
do your own homework		copy a friend's homework
revise a paper several times		revise it just once
volunteer to make a presentation		say you are too nervous to make a presentation
quit school because it's too hard		stay in school even though it is hard

What are some other examples of "taking the easy way out"?

b. Classwork. Read the title of the poem below and study the photograph. Why is graduation an important time in a person's life?

c. Classwork. Look over the poem below. How does it look different from the poem on page 73?

6. Read

Classwork. Read the poem aloud in different ways. For example, you might take turns reading a line aloud.

Jessica Berg

(Graduation)

It's too easy to
      Walk away,
      Sit down,
      Get over.
It's too easy to be
      Cynical,[1]
      Cool,
      Miserable.
It's too easy to turn
      A deaf ear,[2]
      A cold heart,[3]
      A silent voice.
It's too easy to doubt
      Your chances,
      Your future,
      Yourself.
And I never liked nor took the easy way out
So, in a few minutes when they call my name
To come up for the diploma I earned,
I will walk with pride up to the stage.
Easily.

Mel Glenn

[1] **cynical**   negative; seeing only the bad in people and things
[2] **turn a deaf ear**   refuse to listen
[3] **a cold heart**   refuse to feel

About the Author
Mel Glenn is a teacher and poet. Many of his poems are written from the point of view of high school students in the United States.

7. Write-Pair-Share

a. On your own. Choose one or more lines in the poem that interest you. In writing, tell what these lines mean to you.

b. Get together with a partner. Tell your partner what you wrote about. Listen carefully to your partner's ideas.

c. Get together with another pair. Tell them what your partner wrote about.

8. Brainstorm

> *Study Strategy:*
> *Brainstorming*
> See page 163.

Groupwork. Think of different ways to complete the sentence below. Write your ideas on another piece of paper.

It's too easy to _____.

Examples: It's too easy to watch TV instead of doing your homework.

It's too easy to pretend you are sick on the day you must make a presentation.

It's too easy to be lazy.

Read your group's ideas to the class. Together write your own version of the poem.

9. Journal Writing

On your own. Think of a time when you had to choose between taking the easy path and the difficult path. Which path did you choose? Why? What were the consequences of your decision?

Activity Menu

Choose one of the following activities to do.

1. Reader's Theater

Write a Reader's Theater version of the story *Who's Hu?* Assign roles to different classmates and act it out for another class.

2. Read a Novel

Find the novel *Who's Hu?* in a library and read it. Tell your classmates about another event in Emma Hu's life.

3. Make a Career Chart

Choose a career of interest to you. Find out more about this career by looking for information in the library. Try to find answers to these questions:

- What training or education do you need to get a job in this field?

- What special skills does a person in this job need to have?

- Is the number of jobs in this field increasing or decreasing?

Tell your classmates what you learned.

4. Read a Story

Read a story by Nicholasa Mohr. If you like the story, recommend it to your classmates. Tell them why you think they should read it.

5. Interview Your School Guidance Counselor

What does a guidance counselor do? How can this person help you? Invite your school guidance counselor to speak to your class.

6. Explore Careers

Invite someone to your class to talk about his or her career. Before your guest arrives, prepare a list of questions to ask.

7. Find Out More about the Underground Railroad

Think of three things your would like to find out about the Underground Railroad. Then look in the library to find the answers to your questions. Share what you learned with your classmates.

8. Read a Poem

Read another poem by one of the poets in this unit. Recommend one of the poems to your classmates.

Footpath

Path-let . . . leaving home, leading out,
Return my mother to me.
The sun is sinking and darkness coming,
Hens and cocks are already inside and babies drowsing,
Return my mother to me.
We do not have fire-wood and I have not seen the lantern,
There is no more food and the water has run out.
Path-let I pray you, return my mother to me.
Path of the hillocks, path of the small stones,
Path of slipperiness, path of the mud,
Return my mother to me.
Path of the papyrus, path of the rivers,
Path of the small forests, path of the reeds,
Return my mother to me.
Path that winds, path of the short-cut,
Over-trodden path, newly-made path,
Return my mother to me.
Path, I implore you, return my mother to me.
Path of the crossways, path that branches off,
Path of the stinging shrubs, path of the bridge,
Return my mother to me.
Path of the open, path of the valley,
Path of the steep climb, path of the downward slope,
Return my mother to me.
Children are drowsing about to sleep,
Darkness is coming and there is no fire-wood,
And I have not yet found the lantern:
Return my mother to me.

Stella Ngatho
Kenya

Harriet Tubman

Harriet Tubman didn't take no stuff
Wasn't scared of nothing neither
Didn't come in this world to be no slave
And wasn't going to stay one either

"Farewell!" she sang to her friends one night
She was mighty sad to leave 'em
But she ran away that dark, hot night
Ran looking for her freedom

She ran to the woods and she ran through the woods
With the slave catchers right behind her
And she kept on going till she got to the North
Where those mean men couldn't find her

Nineteen times she went back South
To get three hundred others
She ran for her freedom nineteen times
To save black sisters and brothers
Harriet Tubman didn't take no stuff
Wasn't scared of nothing neither
Didn't come in this world to be no slave
And didn't stay one either

And didn't stay one either

Eloise Greenfield

Unit 3:

Have lectures in public schools about understanding different cultures; maybe if someone really knew about someone else's culture then they would know why that person acts different.

11th-grader
Middletown High School
Middletown, R.I.

BREAKING DOWN BARRIERS

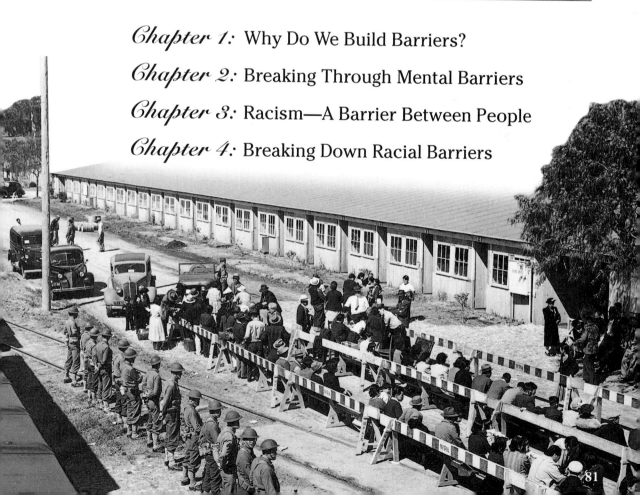

Chapter 1: Why Do We Build Barriers?

*W*hat is a barrier? What purpose do barriers serve? These are two of the questions you will think about in this chapter.

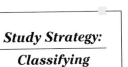

| 1. | **Define** |

Study Strategy:

Classifying

See pages 163–164.

a. Groupwork. These pictures show different kinds of barriers. Use the pictures to help you define the word *barrier*. Write your group's definition on another piece of paper.

b. Compare definitions with the other groups in your class.

c. Look up the word *barrier* in a dictionary and check your definition.

▲▲▲

2. Classify

a. Groupwork. Classify the barriers in Activity 1. Group them in a chart like this:

Natural barriers	Barriers made by people
mountains	dam

Think of other examples to add to your chart.
Then read your ideas to the class.

b. Pairwork. Write your examples of barriers made by people on a chart like this. Then identify the purpose of each barrier.

Barriers made by people

Barrier	Purpose
shower curtain	▪ keeps the water in the shower ▪ prevents the water from getting the floor wet

Get together with another pair. Take turns telling about a barrier on your chart.

3. Preview

Study Strategy:

Previewing

See page 167.

a. Classwork. Look over the short story on pages 86–88. Based on the title and the illustrations, what do you think the story is about?

b. Pairwork. Choose one of the pictures on pages 86–88. What questions could you ask to get more information about the picture? List your ideas in a chart like this:

Example: Picture #1

Questions	Possible Answers
Who is inside the spaceship? *Where is the spaceship from?* *Why is the spaceship coming to Earth?*	

Read your questions to the class. Together think of possible answers to your questions.

 4.   Using Context

Study Strategy:

Using Context

See page 169–170.

a. Classwork. When you read a story, you may come across unfamiliar words. You can make good guesses about the meaning of these words by looking at the context—the words and sentences that come before and after the unfamiliar word. To see how this works, read the paragaph in the box. Use the ideas in the paragraph to help you think of a word or words to write on the line.

> The children were always good during the month of August, especially when it began to get near the twenty-third. It was on this day that the great silver spaceship carrying Professor Hugo's Interplanetary Zoo _____ for its annual six-hour visit to the Chicago area.

Which words and ideas in the paragraph helped you to complete the last sentence?

b. Read the first paragraph of the story "Zoo." What do you think the words *settled down* mean? Which words and ideas in the paragraph helped you guess?

 Language Focus:

Speculating

- Professor Hugo's zoo might travel to different planets.
- It might ___.
- It could ___.

 5.   Predict

Classwork. The story on pages 86–88 takes place in the distant future when it is possible to travel from one planet to another. The name of the zoo in the story is "Professor Hugo's Interplanetary Zoo." What do you think this zoo might be like? How might it be different from a zoo today? List your ideas on the board.

As you read the story, look for answers to your questions from Activity 3.

Zoo

The children were always good during the month of August, especially when it began to get near the twenty-third. It was on this day that the great silver spaceship carrying Professor Hugo's Interplanetary Zoo settled down for its annual six-hour visit to the Chicago area.

Before daybreak the crowds would form, long lines of children and adults both, each one clutching his or her dollar, and waiting with wonderment to see what race of strange creatures[1] the Professor had brought this year.

In the past they had sometimes been treated to three-legged creatures from Venus, or tall, thin men from Mars, or even snakelike horrors[2] from somewhere more distant. This year, as the great round ship settled slowly to earth in the huge tri-city parking area just outside of Chicago, they watched with awe[3] as the sides slowly slid up to reveal the familiar barred cages.

In them were some wild breed[4] of nightmare[5]—small, horselike animals that moved with quick, jerking motions and constantly chattered in a high-pitched tongue. The citizens of Earth

[1]creatures	animals, including people
[2]horrors	things causing fear; scary things
[3]awe	wonder mixed with fear and respect
[4]breed	type
[5]nightmare	frightening dream; something frightening

clustered around as Professor Hugo's crew quickly collected the waiting dollars, and soon the good Professor himself made an appearance, wearing his many-colored rainbow cape and top hat. "Peoples of Earth," he called into his microphone.

The crowd's noise died down and he continued. "Peoples of Earth, this year you see a real treat[6] for your single dollar—the little-known horse-spider people of Kaan—brought to you across a million miles of space at great expense. Gather around, see them, study them, listen to them, tell your friends about them. But hurry! My ship can remain here only six hours!"

And the crowds slowly filed by, at once horrified and fascinated by these strange creatures that looked like horses but ran up the walls of their cages like spiders. "This is certainly worth a dollar," one man remarked, hurrying away. "I'm going home to get the wife."

All day long it went like that, until ten thousand people had filed by the barred cages set into the side of the spaceship. Then, as the six-hour limit ran out, Professor Hugo once more took microphone in hand. "We must go now, but we will return next year on this date. And if you enjoyed our zoo this year, phone your friends in other cities about it. We will land in New York tomorrow, and next week on to London, Paris, Rome, Hong Kong, and Tokyo. Then on to other worlds!"

He waved farewell to them, and as the ship rose from the ground the Earth peoples agreed that this had been the very best Zoo yet. . .

Some two months and three planets later, the silver ship of Professor Hugo settled at last onto the familiar jagged rocks of Kaan, and the queer horse-spider creatures filed quickly out of their cages. Professor Hugo was there to say a few parting words, and then they scurried away in a hundred different directions, seeking their homes among the rocks.

In one, the she-creature was happy to see the return of her mate[7] and offspring.[8] She babbled a greeting in the strange tongue and hurried to embrace[9] them. "It was a long time you were gone. Was it good?"

[6]**treat**   something special that gives pleasure
[7]**mate**   husband or wife, male or female of a pair
[8]**offspring** child or children
[9]**embrace** hug

And the he-creature nodded. "The little one enjoyed it especially. We visited eight worlds and saw many things."

The little one ran up the wall of the cave. "On the place called Earth it was the best. The creatures there wear garments over their skins, and they walk on two legs."

"But isn't it dangerous?" asked the she-creature.

"No," her mate answered. "There are bars to protect us from them. We remain right in the ship. Next time you must come with us. It is well worth the nineteen commocs it costs."

And the little one nodded.
"It was the very best Zoo ever. . . ."

Edward Hoch

About the Author

Edward Hoch has written more than 500 mystery short stories. He also writes material for TV programs.

7. Share Ideas

a. Classwork. Share any answers you found to your questions from Activity 3.

b. Groupwork. Choose one of the questions below to discuss in your group. Ask one person in your group to take notes on your discussion.

1. Think back to your predictions from Activity 5. What do you know about Professor Hugo's zoo now? How is it different from a zoo today?

2. Both the Earth people and the Kaan people paid to go to Professor Hugo's zoo. Why?

3. What was unusual about Professor Hugo's zoo?

4. What was the purpose of the barred cages in Professor Hugo's zoo? Who do you think the bars were protecting?

5. What does this story say to you about barriers?

Report your group's ideas to the class.

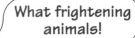

8. Interpret

a. Classwork. Describe Professor Hugo's Interplanetary Zoo from two points of view. First tell what you think the Kaan people are thinking and feeling at Professor Hugo's zoo. Then tell what the Earth people might be thinking and feeling.

> What frightening animals!

> How strange. They're wearing garments!

Kaan people	Earth people

b. Pairwork. Use the ideas in your diagram to write a conversation between two people at Professor Hugo's zoo. First decide if your conversation is between two Earth people or two Kaan people. Then write your conversation.

Example: Person A: What do you think of the zoo?

  Person B: It's incredible. What weird animals!

  Person A: _____

c. Pairwork. Read your conversation aloud to the class. Let your classmates guess where the two people are from.

9. Define

a. Classwork. The sentences below are from the story "Zoo." Were you able to use context to guess the meaning of the underlined words? Read the sentences and complete a chart like this:

Word from the story	Guess from context	Helpful context clues
clutching *chattered* *garments*		

Sentences from the Story

1. Before daybreak the crowds would form, long lines of children and adults both, each one <u>clutching</u> his or her dollar . . .

2. In the cages were small, horselike animals that moved with quick, jerking motions and constantly <u>chattered</u> in a high-pitched tongue.

3. "On the place called Earth it was the best. The creatures there wear <u>garments</u> over their skins, and they walk on two legs."

b. Look up each word in a dictionary and check your guesses.

Language Focus:

Guessing

- I think the word *clutching* means "holding."
- The word *clutching* probably means something like "holding."

10. Write

a. Classwork. In Unit 2, you read a Reader's Theater about people on the Underground Railroad. Below, is the first part of a Reader's Theater based on the short story "Zoo." Look over the cast of the play. Where do the two scenes take place? What is the setting of each scene?

b. Listen to the first part of Scene 1 and read along.

The Zoo

A Reader's Theater based on the story by Edward Hoch

Cast, Scene 1
Professor Hugo
First Earth Person
Second Earth Person
First Kaan Person
Second Kaan Person
First Narrator
Second Narrator

Cast, Scene 2
She-creature of Kaan
He-creature of Kaan
Young child of Kaan
Professor Hugo
First Narrator
Second Narrator

SCENE 1

First Narrator: It's daybreak in August, sometime in the distant future. Outside the city of Chicago, a line of people is forming in a large parking area.

Second Narrator: Suddenly a large spaceship appears above the crowd of people.

First Earth Person: There it is. There's Professor Hugo's Zoo.

Second Earth Person: What do you think he brought?

First Earth Person: I can't imagine. Did you see the zoo last year?

Second Earth Person: With the three-legged creatures from Mars? They were terrifying!

First Narrator: The spaceship slowly descends to Earth and lands in the parking area.

Second Narrator: The sides of the spaceship slide up to reveal barred cages.

Second Earth Person:

---

c. Groupwork. What happens next in the play? Finish Scene 1 and write a Scene 2. Take turns recording your group's ideas.

d. Groupwork. Practice reading your play aloud. Some people in your group can take two roles.

e. Type your play into a computer or handwrite it so that your classmates can read it easily. Then make copies of your play.

f. Get together with another group. Choose roles and practice reading each group's play.

g. Tape record both versions of the play or perform your plays for the class.

Chapter 2: Breaking Through Mental Barriers

*M*ental barriers can make it difficult to give a speech, take a test, or learn to do something new. But according to sports counselor Marlin Mackenzie, you can learn how to overcome these barriers.

 1. **Interpret**

Classwork. What are these people thinking? How might their thoughts act as a barrier? Share ideas with your classmates.

 2. **Journal Writing**

On your own. Imagine yourself giving a speech to your classmates. Describe the picture that you see in your mind. As you write, think about the questions below.

- What do you see yourself doing as you give your speech?
- How do you feel?
- How are your classmates reacting to your speech?

3. ▶ Preview

a. Pairwork. Look over the article on pages 93–94. Read the first sentence in the first four paragraphs. Then write a question based on the information in each sentence.

Example: *What was the pole-vaulter's problem?*

b. Read your questions to the class. Together think of possible answers to your questions. Then tell what you think the article is about.

4. ▶ Read

On your own. As you read the article, look for answers to your questions from Activity 3.

Breaking Mental Barriers

from *Science Digest*

1   A young pole-vaulter had a problem. Time after time he would sprint down the track, place his pole and leap for the crossbar. Time after time, he sailed into the bar, not over it. The harder he tried, the more his body seemed drawn into the bar, like a nail to a magnet. He knew how to vault; he just had a mental block that kept him from doing it.

2   Now he's competing successfully again, thanks to Marlin Mackenzie, head of the sports-counselor training program at Columbia University Teachers College. Mackenzie is one of a growing number of professionals being consulted by athletes whose performance problems have a psychological basis.[1] And there is a growing realization that crippling mental barriers of all sorts can be overcome, whether they involve hitting a golf ball or giving a speech, taking a test or talking to the boss.

3   "Any given goal has a strategy," says Mackenzie, "a mental 'map' of the best way to reach that goal. The map will often be largely subconscious,[2] and it is usually a complicated set of sensory images—pictures, sounds, physical

[1] **a psychological basis**   come from one's mind
[2] **subconscious**   in the mind but not consciously known

sensations—mixed with emotional images." In the case of the pole-vaulter, Mackenzie elicited the images that raced through the young man's mind in the split second it took to spring from ground to crossbar. "He was talking to himself, trying to get himself through the jump by 'hearing' words of encouragement. But words are too slow. He needed an image that would distract his mind from the task. His body knew how to jump—his brain had just forgotten that he knew."

4   Mackenzie told the vaulter not to think about jumping, but to think of the sound of his pole hitting the ground as the first note of a love song. The strategy worked almost the first time he had the chance to use it.

5   Is there anything the average person can do to break through a mental barrier? According to Mackenzie, a positive mental image of the goal successfully attained[3] is crucial.[4] "If I say, 'don't think about pink elephants,' what's the first thing you think of?" he asks. "If you go into a job interview telling yourself not to stumble over your words, you picture the mistake—and often commit[5] it. But if you picture yourself speaking clearly and well, your subconscious is channeled into the right groove and you're likely to live up to[6] that picture."

---

[3]**attained**   reached, accomplished
[4]**crucial**   extremely important; of the greatest importance
[5]**commit**   make, do
[6]**live up to** act like

5. Share Ideas

a. Pairwork. Choose one of the questions below to discuss with your partner. Take notes on your discussion.

1. How can mental barriers cause problems?
2. How did Marlin Mackenzie help the pole-vaulter compete successfully?
3. How could you use the ideas in this article?
4. According to Mackenzie, what should you picture yourself doing before you give a speech?

b. Find another pair of students in your class who discussed the same question. Exchange ideas.

c. Tell the class which question you chose and report on your discussion.

6. Use Context

a. On your own. Were you able to use context to define these words from the article? Look back at the reading to find the words and write your guesses. Then answer each question.

1. Paragraph #**1**: *mental block*
   Definition: _a barrier in your mind; a way of think-_
   ing that stops you from doing something
   What do you have a mental block against doing?

   _____

2. Paragraph #**3**: *mental map*
   Definition: _____
   What can a mental map help you to do?

   _____

> **Study Strategy:**
> **Using Context**
> See page 169–170.

3. Paragraph #**3**: *sensory image*

Definition: _____

Imagine yourself doing something. What sensory images come to mind?

_____

4. Paragraph #**3**: *words of encouragement*

Definition: _____

Write a sentence with words of encouragement. When might you say this sentence to yourself?

_____

b. Compare ideas with a partner. Then, share your definitions and answers with your classmates.

7. **Apply**

Groupwork. What advice do you think Marlin Mackenzie would give these people? Write your group's ideas on another piece of paper.

1. A student is having trouble taking tests. Before a test, she tells herself, "Don't be nervous."
2. A young man is trying to learn to swim. The night before he goes swimming, he lies in bed thinking about the next day. In his mind, he sees himself sinking in the water.
3. A businessperson has to give a speech to a large group of people, and she is worried about forgetting what to say and speaking too quickly.

Compare ideas with your classmates.

8. **Journal Writing**

a. On your own. Think about the information in the article "Breaking Mental Barriers." Then imagine yourself giving a speech to the whole school. Draw or describe the picture that you see in your mind. How is this picture different from the picture you described in Activity 2?

b. Think of something you have a mental block against doing. How might you use the information in the article to overcome this mental block? Write your ideas in your journal.

9. Write

On your own. Think about something difficult that you have done. How did you feel? What thoughts went through your mind? What helped you do this difficult thing? In writing, share your experience with your classmates. Here are some ideas to get started:

1. With a group of classmates, brainstorm a set of things that are difficult to do. Record your group's ideas.

   Examples: move to a new country
   learn to play a new sport
   walk away from a fight
   say that you made a mistake

Look over your group's ideas. Which of these ideas makes you think of something from your experience? Is it something you want to write about?

2. Complete these sentences in different ways.

   Examples:

   I had a difficult time *making new friends when I moved here.*

   It was hard for me to *understand the language when I*

   came here.

Look over the ideas you wrote down.
Is there something you want to write about?

3. Look over your notes for #1 and #2 and choose an experience to write about. Be sure to choose something that you feel comfortable sharing with your classmates.

4. Think about the experience you chose and quickwrite in your journal for five minutes.

5. Read your quickwriting aloud to a classmate. Find out what your classmate would like to know more about.

6. Write a first draft of your paper.

7. Refer to the Writer's Guide on pages 174–175 for ideas about revising your paper.

> ***Study Strategy:***
> ***Brainstorming***
> See page 163.

> ***Study Strategy:***
> ***Quickwriting***
> See page 168.

Chapter 3: Racism—A Barrier Between People

*R*acism is a barrier because it prevents people from getting to know each other; it causes people to fear and hate those who are different.

1. **Listen**

a. Classwork. The article on pages 100–101 deals with the treatment of Japanese Americans before and during the Second World War. According to the article, racism against Japanese Americans had a long history in the United States. Listen for the examples of racism in this paragraph from the reading. List them on another piece of paper.

WE DON'T WANT ANY JAPS BACK HERE--EVER!

b. Listen again and then compare notes with your classmates.

2. Predict

Classwork. In 1942, the U.S. government forced nearly 120,000 people to leave their homes and businesses and to move to internment camps. These internment camps were really prisons. All of the people forced to move were of Japanese ancestry. What reasons can you think of to explain the government's action?

▲ *Japanese detainees await barracks assignments.*

3. Read

On your own. Read to check your predictions from Activity 2.

A Shameful Chapter

(Part 1)

by Barbara Rogasky

1   On December 7, 1941, Japanese planes bombed the Pearl Harbor Naval Base in the Hawaiian Islands and destroyed most of the U.S. Pacific fleet.[1] In a few days America was at war with Japan and her allies, Germany and Italy.

2   The lives of most people with German and Italian backgrounds who lived in America did not change much because of the war. The Japanese were not so lucky.

3   Nearly all 120,000 Japanese living on the West Coast spent the war years locked up behind barbed wire[2] and under armed guard. Two thirds of them were American citizens.

4   The real reason seems simple. German Americans and Italian Americans were Caucasian. They were white. But the Japanese were not. That was enough to suspect each and every one of being a spy.[3]

5   Racism against the Japanese had a long history here. The *Issei*, those born in Japan but living in the United States, were not allowed to own land. Nor were they ever permitted to become American citizens, no matter how long they lived here. They, and their American-born children, called *Nisei*, were stoned[4] in the streets. Many restaurants refused to serve them, barbers would not cut their hair, homeowners would not sell or rent to them. Hand painted signs announced JAPS KEEP MOVING—THIS IS A WHITE MAN'S NEIGHBORHOOD.

[1]**fleet**	group of warships
[2]**barbed wire**	wire with sharp points attached to it
[3]**spy**	person employed by a country to find secret information about another country
[4]**stoned**	hit by stones thrown at them

6   When the war started, rumors[5] flew. Japanese were said to be radioing war planes about to bomb the coast. Japanese farmers burning brush were accused of lighting "arrows of fire," directing enemy aircraft to important targets. Japanese even were blamed for sabotaging[6] power lines that were actually broken by cows scratching their backs on poles.

7   No evidence[7] of spying or sabotage was ever found, then or at any time during the war. Yet, on February 19, 1942, President Franklin Roosevelt signed Executive Order 9066. It allowed the army to call sections of the country "military areas." Any person or group could be kept out of those areas if the army thought it necessary.

8   The West Coast was already officially a war zone. Lieutenant General John L. DeWitt, chief of the Western Defense Command, issued the first "Civilian Exclusion Orders." He intended to move out anyone he believed threatened the region's security.[8] Soon all people of Japanese ancestry were forced to leave their homes.

9   The Japanese were given as little as one week's notice. They had to leave everything behind and sell what they could for whatever they could get. They were cheated in countless[9] ways—by those who paid twenty-five dollars for a new car and three hundred dollars for a house, and by the U.S. Government, which promised to protect Japanese property but used it or disposed of it without offering compensation[10] of any kind. The government promised to keep cars owned by the Japanese until the end of the war, and then took them for its own use without paying a penny.

[5]**rumors**	information, often false, spread from person to person
[6]**sabotaging**	damaging on purpose
[7]**evidence**	proof
[8]**security**	safety
[9]**countless**	more than can be counted; very many
[10]**compensation**	payment

4. ◆ Review

a. Classwork. Look back at your predictions from Activity 2. Do any of your ideas match the information given in the reading?

b. Pairwork. Check your understanding of the passage. Look back at each paragraph. What questions does the paragraph answer? For each paragraph, write one question. Then write the answer to the question.

Example:

Paragraph #	Question	Answer
1	*What happened on December 7, 1941?*	*Japan bombed U.S. ships in Hawaii.*

c. Classwork. Take turns asking and answering questions about the information in the passage.

d. Classwork. Did you find this activity helpful? If so, how did it help you?

5. ◆ Read

Classwork. Think of three things you would like to find out in the next part of the reading. On the board, list your ideas as questions. Then look for answers to your questions as you read Part 2.

A Shameful Chapter
(Part 2)

10   **N**o one told the Japanese where they were going. Loaded onto trains and buses, they were taken to "assembly centers." These were sometimes stockyards[1] or stables,[2] stinking and dirty. Each family was given a table, a chair, cots, and mattresses and straw to stuff them with. Everyone was kept under armed guard at all times.

11   In a few months the Japanese were moved again—this time to Camp Jerome in Arkansas, Camp Manzanar in the California desert, Camp Poston in Arizona, and to seven more camps miles from the West Coast. These were terrible places. It could get as hot as 120 degrees and as cold as below zero. The wind- and sand-storms were severe.[3]

12   The Japanese found unfinished wooden barracks[4] at the camps. Each barrack was divided into four or six rooms. Here, each family was given one twenty-by-twenty foot space, which contained a potbellied stove, one bare bulb hanging from the ceiling, cots, and blankets. That was all.

13   These places were called internment camps. They were really prisons. The Japanese were fenced in, the gates were locked, and they were watched twenty-four hours a day. According to American law, people may not be arrested and imprisoned unless there is some evidence of a crime. They are then considered innocent until proven guilty by a judge or jury using the evidence as proof. Then—and only then—may a resident or citizen be sentenced to a period of time under lock and

[1]**stockyards**   places where large groups of cattle or other animals are kept for a short time
[2]**stables**   places where horses are kept
[3]**severe**   hard, harsh
[4]**barracks**   buildings designed to house soldiers

key. The Japanese were denied[5] these rights. The American government had broken its own law.

14   Ironically, in February 1943, the *Nisei* were allowed to be drafted into the army. Many eventually formed the 442nd Regimental Combat team. By the end of the war in Europe, this group of thirty-three thousand men had won more military honors than any other unit in the entire U.S. armed forces. Their families remained imprisoned.

15   The Japanese began to be released from the camps in January 1945. The war ended for good[6] in August 1945, but the last internment camp was not closed until March 1946.

16   Gradually, several groups and individuals began pressuring the government to admit that it had violated the Constitution by interning the Japanese. In 1983, a government committee published a report called *Personal Justice Denied.* It admitted that the law had been broken and called for the government to apologize and make some payment to the Japanese who had been forced into camps.

17   Five years later, the government agreed. It would pay twenty thousand dollars to each person from the camps who was still alive. Every payment would come with a letter of apology from the president. By then, it was forty-six years after the camps had opened, and half of the original 120,000 had died.

18   The first payments were made on October 9, 1990. A personal letter of apology from President George Bush came with each check.

19   But are the money and the apology enough? No apology or payment can make what happened less wrong. Only one thing can begin to right[7] this shameful chapter in our history. We must remember it. Because nothing like it must ever happen again.

▲ *Former President George Bush*

[5]**denied**   not allowed to have
[6]**for good** forever
[7]**right**   correct

6. Share Ideas

Groupwork. Here are some questions you can discuss in your group.

1. What thoughts and questions came to mind as you read the article? Point to specific lines in the article and explain your reaction.

2. Why do you think this article is titled "A Shameful Chapter"? What does the title mean to you?

3. Reread the last paragraph of the article. Do you agree with the writer? Why or why not?

4. How did racism against Japanese Americans act as a barrier?

7. Take Notes

a. Classwork. Share any answers you found to your questions from Activity 5. Show where in the passage you found the answers.

b. Pairwork. Look back over Parts 1 and 2 of the reading to find information about each topic listed in the chart below. Identify the paragraph with information about each topic. In your own words, note the important details about each topic.

> **Study Strategy:**
>
> **Taking Notes in a Chart**
>
> See page 169.

Topic	Paragraphs	Details
▪ rumors against Japanese	6, 7	rumors said Japanese Americans were helping Japan—directing Japanese planes, sabotaging power lines; rumors were untrue
▪ Executive Order 9066		
▪ how the Japanese were cheated		
▪ internment camps		
▪ the 442nd Regimental Combat team		
▪ apologizing to the Japanese		

c. Get together with a partner and compare charts. Then share information from your chart with the class.

Language Focus:

Expressing Opinions

■ We think the first statement is false because . . .

■ We believe the second statement is ___ because . . .

8. **Give Examples**

a. Pairwork. Decide if the following statements are true or false. Then give details and examples to support or refute each statement. Write your ideas on a chart like this:

	True	False	Details/Examples
1. Japanese Americans helped direct Japanese war planes to important targets in the United States.			
2. People of Japanese ancestry were cheated when they had to leave their homes and businesses quickly.			
3. The internment camps were comfortable places in which to live.			
4. Immediately after the war, the U.S. government apologized to the Japanese who had been forced into camps.			

b. Share ideas with your classmates.

9. **Listen**

a. Classwork. You are going to hear some information about the internment of Japanese Americans during World War II. Before you listen to the tape, read the questions below. Then listen for answers to the questions and take notes on another piece of paper.

1. According to this passage, rumors that Japanese Americans were helping the enemy led to mistreatment of Japanese Americans. What examples does the passage give?

2. Japanese Americans suffered heavy losses when they were forced to leave their homes and businesses quickly. What example does the passage give?

b. Compare ideas with your classmates.

10. Journal Writing

a. On your own. Why do you think racism exists? As you write your ideas in your journal, think about racism against Japanese Americans before and during the Second World War. Think also of examples of racism you have read or heard about. Explore your answer to the question as you write in your journal.

b. Get together with your classmates and share ideas from your journal writing.

11. Preview

a. Classwork. Read the title of the poem on page 108. What do you already know about Executive Order 9066? Based on the title, what do you think the poem is about?

b. The narrator of this poem is a Japanese American teenager. How do you think Executive Order 9066 might have affected her? Share ideas with your classmates.

12. Shared Reading

Groupwork. Read this poem aloud in different ways. For example, you might take turns reading a sentence aloud.

Language Focus:

Speculating about Past Events

- She might have been forced to move to an internment camp.

- She might have —— .

IN RESPONSE TO EXECUTIVE ORDER 9066:
ALL AMERICANS OF JAPANESE DESCENT MUST
REPORT TO RELOCATION CENTERS

Dear Sirs:
Of course I'll come. I've packed my galoshes[1]
and three packets of tomato seeds. Denise calls them
"love apples." My father says where we're going
they won't grow.

I am a fourteen-year-old girl with bad spelling
and a messy room. If it helps any, I will tell you
I have always felt funny using chopsticks
and my favorite food is hot dogs.
My best friend is a white girl named Denise —
we look at boys together. She sat in front of me
all through grade school because of our names:
O'Connor, Ozawa. I know the back of Denise's head very well.

I tell her she's going bald. She tells me I copy on tests.
We're best friends.

I saw Denise today in Geography class.
She was sitting on the other side of the room.
"You're trying to start a war," she said, "giving secrets away
to the Enemy. Why can't you keep your big mouth shut?"

I didn't know what to say.
I gave her a packet of tomato seeds
and asked her to plant them for me, told her
when the first tomato ripened
she'd miss me.

Dwight Okita

About the Author

Dwight Okita was born in
1958. He now lives in
Chicago where he writes
poems and makes videos.

[1]**galoshes**   waterproof overshoes

13. Share Ideas

a. Groupwork. What is your reaction to the poem? Share ideas with the people in your group. Here are some other questions you can discuss.

1. What information does the narrator of the poem give about herself?
   List what you know about her.
2. How is the narrator similar to and different from her classmates?
3. How does Denise's behavior towards the narrator change?
   Why do you think this happens?
4. What does this poem say to you about barriers?

b. Share ideas from your discussion with your classmates.

14. Write

On your own. Write a diary entry from the point of view of the narrator of the poem. Choose one specific day in the narrator's life. Then tell what happened on this day and describe your (the narrator's) reaction.

Diary/Date

Chapter 4: Breaking Down Racial Barriers

*W*hat can be done to break down the barriers between people of different races and cultures? In this chapter, you will read about a program in New York that is bringing together students from different cultural backgrounds. You will also find out what teenagers from around the United States have to say about breaking down racial barriers.

Study Strategy:

Brainstorming

See page 163.

1. ▷ Brainstorm

Classwork. What comes to mind when you hear the words *racial barriers*? Write your ideas on the board.

2. ▷ Preview

a. Pairwork. Read the title and the first sentence of the magazine article on page 111. What is your answer to the question at the beginning of the article? Why?

Study Strategy:

Previewing

See page 167.

b. The magazine article on page 111 is about the Peace Games, which bring teenagers together to play basketball. The teenagers, who are from different cultures and communities, must get along and work together to win a basketball game. Before you read the article, think of possible answers to the questions below.

1. Why were the Peace Games started?
2. What is the purpose of the Peace Games?
3. What effects have the Peace Games had?

3. ▷ Read

As you read the article, look for answers to the questions from Activity 2.

Aiming for Peace

Can a simple game of hoops[1] bring together two totally different cultures and communities?

People in Brooklyn, New York, think so. And they have some results to prove it.

For years, Hasidic Jews and African-Americans have lived side by side with one another in the Crown Heights section of Brooklyn. But they have never bothered to learn much about one another.

In 1991, violent riots[2] broke out after a young African-American was killed by a Hasidic driver. Soon after, a Hasidic man was stabbed to death.[3]

The two groups became bitter enemies. That's when community leaders started CURE, a program to bring together teens

from both groups. CURE stands for Communication, Understanding, Respect, and Education.

A central part of CURE is the Peace Games. In the Peace Games, Hasidic and African-American teens meet on the basketball court. The teams consist of youths from both communities. To win a game, these teens must learn how to play together and get along.

"Before, we would just say Hasidic people were different without trying to understand why," says Sean Joe, 24. "It was surprising to find out we had things in common—like basketball, music, and a love of good food."

At first, Yudi Simon had his doubts. He and his father had been attacked by a

---

[1] **hoops**	basketball
[2] **riots**	violent disorder by a large group of people
[3] **stabbed to death**	killed with a knife

group of Crown Heights youths during the riots. His father had been stabbed in the leg. So Yudi, 16, wasn't sure what to expect.

"As soon as I started to play, though, I saw how effective basketball was," he says. "In order to play basketball, you have to trust your teammates. You need to use teamwork. These are the same skills you need in order to get along."

Since the first basketball games were played, the groups have gotten together to paint a mural, plant trees, and even form an interracial rap group.

The results have been good. The violence has stopped. And Yudi says he meets kids from the program all the time.

"You see someone you know from playing basketball, and you go say hello and talk," he says. "That never happened here before."

Scott Brodeur

Language Focus:

Relating Cause and Effect

- One effect of the Peace Games was that the teenagers learned more about each other.
- The Peace Games resulted in . . .
- Because of the Peace Games, . . .
- Due to the Peace Games, . . .

 4. **Review**

a. Pairwork. Share answers to the questions from Activity 2.

b. Classwork. What effects did the Peace Games have? List your ideas in a tree diagram on the board.

Effects
- teenagers learned more about each other
- they started talking to each other

 5. **Design**

a. Classwork. Why is basketball a good way to break down barriers between people? List your ideas on the board.

In order to play basketball, you have to _____.

If you want to win a basketball game, you must _____.

Basketball is a good way to bring people together because _____.

b. Groupwork. Basketball is one way to break down barriers. In your group, think of another way to bring together people from different cultures. Then tell why you think it is a good way to bring people together.

c. Share your group's idea with the class.

6. ▷ Preview

a. Classwork. Look over the reading on pages 114–115. Who are the writers? What is their purpose in writing?

b. Classwork. Here is one student's answer to the question, *What can individuals do to bring about greater understanding between different racial and ethnic groups?* What suggestions does this student make?

> People should start being educated about other races at an early age so that when they come in contact with these people later they will act kindly toward them. Younger people should be brought up to believe that all races are equal. World geography classes should deal more than they do now with races. Foreign history courses should also be available. These courses would give kids an understanding of other cultures so when they meet people from these cultures they know how to react. People should also be educated about the great mistakes prejudice has caused in history. Example: The Holocaust.
>
> *Eighth-grader*
> *Laramie Jr. High School*
> *Laramie, Wy.*

Language Focus:

Reporting Another Person's Ideas

- This student says that schools should teach children about different races.
- This student suggests that . . ..
- According to the student from Laramie, ...

7. ▷ Jigsaw Reading

a. Groupwork. Each person in your group can choose a different answer to read. As you read, look for the student's suggestions. List them on another piece of paper.

What can individuals do to bring about greater understanding between different racial and ethnic groups?

1

Have lectures in public schools about understanding different cultures; maybe if someone really knew about someone else's culture then they would know why that person acts different.

11th-grader
Middletown High School
Middletown, R.I.

2

Expose children at an early age to different racial and ethnic groups. All through a child's elementary years and high school years, other cultures must be taught in school. If someone is referring to another racial or ethnic group in a negative way tell them how you feel about it. Remaining silent only allows them to think that you believe the same.

11th-grader
Craig High School
Janesville, Wis.

3

For a greater understanding there should be more ads like the ones on MTV that say 'Paper is to recycle (people aren't).' And make more ads with deeper meaning on how to stop prejudice. For example, The Olympics: A Cartoon Ad: A man from Angola is dribbling the basketball, passes it behind his back, and it's picked up by a Chinese who spins it on his finger. Then he passes it to a man from Lithuania, who dribbles between his legs than alleyoops it to Scottie Pippen, who hammers a dunk. He breaks the backboard, and everything is black, and the basketball is sitting there and has a picture of the World on it.

Eighth-grader / Laramie Jr. High School / Laramie, Wyoming

4

I think that individuals need to start getting more involved with the people around them. Learn how to be friendly and get out and meet people. Big, small, fat and tall. It shouldn't matter. These days, kids just need to learn to be open! Kids also need the encouragment of their parents. That right there might be what is really holding the whole process back.

11th-grader
Meridian Independent
School District
Meridian, Texas

5

We can intermix; people who need public housing can also live in the suburbs so the city won't be known as the only place where all the black, Hispanic, and other races live. We should also have groups that encourage people to be proud of who they are. We should encourage people to at least try to like a racial group they dislike for one day.

Seventh-grader / Visitation Academy / St. Louis, Missouri

6

Make sure more classes and areas are racially mixed. Teach children about prejudice at an earlier age and make it clear to them that it is not good. Stop teaching prejudice at home. Learn to settle any disputes without violence and insults.

Eighth-grader • Placerita Jr. High School • Newhall, California

b. Groupwork. Take turns reporting the suggestions. Choose one person in your group to record all of the suggestions.

c. Groupwork. Look over the list of suggestions. Put a plus sign (+) next to the two suggestions you like best. Tell why you think they are good ideas. Then report your group's ideas to the class.

8. Write a Letter

What can your school do to bring about greater understanding between different racial and ethnic groups? Write a letter to your school principal with your suggestions.

Activity Menu

1. Why Build Barriers?

Research a barrier built by people. Find out why it was built and what purpose it served or serves. Collect pictures to show your classmates and tell them what you learned.

2. Take Photographs

Take photographs of different kinds of barriers in your area. Display your pictures with captions identifying the purpose of each barrier.

3. Professor Hugo's Zoo

Imagine Professor Hugo's zoo the following year. What happens when he brings the zoo to Earth? In writing, tell your story of the zoo.

4. Two Points of View

Think of a disagreement you had with another person. Describe the disagreement from your point of view. Then put yourself in the other person's shoes and describe his or her point of view.

5. Set a Goal

Think of something you hope to accomplish in the future. Picture yourself reaching your goal and describe the picture you see in your mind.

6. Write a Diary Entry

What was life like in the internment camps? Look for descriptions of living conditions in one of the camps. Based on the information you collect, write a diary entry from the point of view of someone living in the camp.

7. Overcoming Obstacles

Look for biographical information about Langston Hughes or Sandra Cisneros. Find out about an obstacle they faced and what they accomplished in spite of this obstacle.

As I Grew Older

by Langston Hughes

It was a long time ago.
I have almost forgotten my dream.
But it was there then,
In front of me,
Bright like a sun—
My dream.

And then the wall rose,
Rose slowly,
Slowly,
Between me and my dream.
Rose slowly, slowly,
Dimming,
Hiding,
The light of my dream.
Rose until it touched the sky—
The wall.

Shadow.
I am black.

I lie down in the shadow.
No longer the light of my dream before me,
Above me.
Only the thick wall.
Only the shadow.

My hands!
My dark hands!
Break through the wall!
Find my dream!
Help me to shatter this darkness,
To smash this night,
To break this shadow
Into a thousand lights of sun,
Into a thousand whirling dreams
Of sun!

Those Who Don't
by Sandra Cisneros

Those who don't know any better come into our neighborhood scared. They think we're dangerous. They think we will attack them with shiny knives. They are stupid people who are lost and got here by mistake.

But we aren't afraid. We know the guy with the crooked eye is Davey the Baby's brother, and the tall one next to him in the straw brim,[1] that's Rosa's Eddie V. and the big one that looks like a dumb grown man, he's Fat Boy, though he's not fat anymore nor a boy.

All brown all around, we are safe. But watch us drive into a neighborhood of another color and our knees go shakity-shake and our car windows get rolled up tight and our eyes look straight. Yeah. That is how it goes and goes.

[1]**brim** hat

Unit 4:

CROSSING BRIDGES

119

Chapter 1: Bridge Designs

1. **Share a Poem**

a. Classwork. Look at the bridge in the painting. Which part of the world do you think the painting is from? Is the bridge design similar to any bridges you have seen before?

b. Read the poem. Where do you think the young woman was going? Why?

Nàng thì dặm khách xa-xăm,   Far, far away she was going
Bạc phan cầu giá,   Across frost-covered bridges
đen rầm ngàn mây   Toward an unknown land

Nguyễn Du from The Tale of Kieu, *1813*

2.

Journal Writing

Think about a bridge you often use or one that you remember well. Write about it in your journal. Draw a sketch of the bridge and describe it in as much detail as you can.

3. Construct an Arch

Materials: *for each team, 1 sheet of graph paper, 2 sheets of construction paper, scissors, two large hardcover textbooks of equal size, 2 sheets of 8.5 × 11 inch paper*

Pairwork. Look at the bridge in the picture. What is its basic design? Your task is to design an arch with shapes you will cut from paper. Follow the instructions on pages 122–123.

Step 1: Make a sketch of the basic design.

Step 2: Look at the shapes below. Draw the same three shapes on your sheet of graph paper. Cut them out. These shapes are the patterns for making your basic arch blocks.

A

B

C

Step 3: You will need a total of 13 blocks. Decide how many blocks from each shape you will need to make an arch design. Place your graph paper patterns on the construction paper and use a pencil to outline enough blocks to lay out your arch.

Step 4: Cut your blocks out of the construction paper. Arrange them on a flat surface in the shape of an arch.

Step 5: Discuss each of these questions with your partner. Take notes on your answers:

a. How did you plan your design?

b. How did you decide how many of each shape you needed?

Hint:
You will need only one of shape C

Step 6: Compare an arch bridge design with a simple flat beam design.

a. Set up two hardcover texbooks of the same size on a flat surface about eight inches apart. Place a flat sheet of plain 8.5 x 11 inch paper (not construction paper) across the two ends. Place a paper clip in the center of the paper. Observe what happens.

b. Bend the paper in the shape of an arch and fix it between the two books. Brace the ends of the paper against the book bindings, as shown in the illustration. Tape a paper clip to the center of the paper arch. Observe what happens.

c. Compare the strength of the two designs. Which one is stronger? Why?

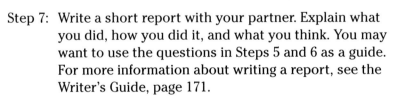

Step 7: Write a short report with your partner. Explain what you did, how you did it, and what you think. You may want to use the questions in Steps 5 and 6 as a guide. For more information about writing a report, see the Writer's Guide, page 171.

First, we made a sketch of the basic design.
Next...

4. Identify

a. On your own. You have already considered two types of basic bridge design: the **arch** and the **simple beam**. The drawings below illustrate two more complex bridge designs. How are they different from the simple forms?

cantilever ▼

suspension ▲

b. Look at these photographs and drawings. Identify the type of bridge design for each. Compare your answers with those of a classmate.

Old London Bridge, c. 1750 ▶

FLUVIUS

South warke

▲ Quebec Bridge

◀ Vermont covered
bridge

Bridges over a
Peruvian River,
c. 1752 ▶

The Brooklyn Bridge, completed 1883

a. Classwork. Discuss the bridge in this photograph. What does the information in the box tell you about it? What is its basic design?

b. Write a short description of the Brooklyn Bridge based on the photograph and the facts in the box. Add more information from other sources if you want to.

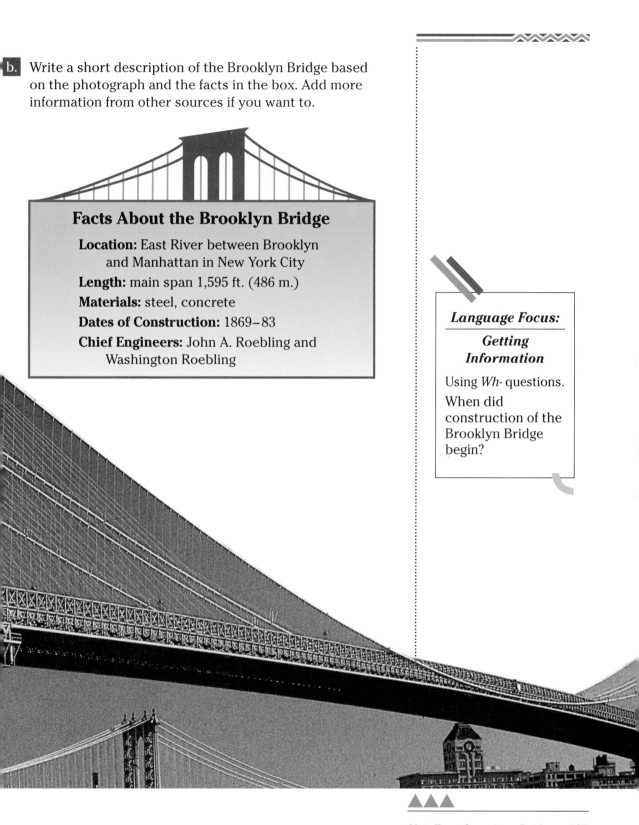

Facts About the Brooklyn Bridge

Location: East River between Brooklyn and Manhattan in New York City

Length: main span 1,595 ft. (486 m.)

Materials: steel, concrete

Dates of Construction: 1869–83

Chief Engineers: John A. Roebling and Washington Roebling

Language Focus:

Getting Information

Using *Wh-* questions.
When did construction of the Brooklyn Bridge begin?

Chapter 2: Facing Change

*B*ecause bridges make it possible to move from one place to another, they often symbolize change. Sometimes people have to leave a place or make a change in their lives whether they want to or not. In this chapter, you will think and read about facing these kinds of changes.

1. Brainstorm

Groupwork. Think of some changes you have already faced in your life. What other changes do you think you will face in the future? List your ideas on another piece of paper.

Examples: moving to a new place to live

having a new brother or sister

going to a new school

Study Strategy:

Brainstorming

See page 164.

---

2. Quickwrite

a. On your own. Think about a time when you had to leave a place or start something new. Quickwrite for five minutes about your experience.

b. Pairwork. Read your quickwriting aloud to a partner. Invite your partner to ask questions about the details. Then work with your partner to make notes on the right side of an experience chart like this.

What happened?	
How did you feel about it then?	
How do you feel about it now?	

c. Groupwork. Get together with another pair. Tell your partner's story.

Classwork. The story you are going to read was written by Ernest Hemingway. The photographs below give you some ideas about the author's life. What do they tell you about him? Discuss each item before you read the story. What can you conclude about Ernest Hemingway? What kind of person was he? What did he write about?

A Pictorial Biography of Ernest Hemingway (1899-1961)

THE SUN ALSO RISES

Daily Press

Bloody Civil War Breaks Out in S...

Fascis...
Republica...
Governm...

THE OLD MAN AT THE BRIDGE

by Ernest Hemingway

An old man with steel rimmed spectacles[1] and very dusty clothes sat by the side of the road. There was a pontoon bridge across the river and carts, trucks, and men, women and children were crossing it. The mule-drawn carts staggered[2] up the steep bank from the bridge with soldiers helping push against the spokes of the wheels. The trucks ground up and away heading out of it all and the peasants[3] plodded along in the ankle deep dust. But the old man sat there without moving. He was too tired to go any farther.

"Where do you come from?" I asked him.

"From San Carlos,[4]" he said, and smiled.

That was his native town and so it gave him pleasure to mention it and he smiled.

"I was taking care of animals," he explained.

"Oh," I said, not quite understanding.

"Yes," he said, "I stayed, you see, taking care of animals. I was the last one to leave the town of San Carlos."

He did not look like a shepherd nor a herdsman and I looked at his black dusty clothes and his gray dusty face and his steel rimmed spectacles and said, "What animals were they?"

"Various animals," he said, and shook his head. "I had to leave them."

I was watching the bridge and the African looking country of the Ebro Delta[5] and

[1]**spectacles**   eyeglasses
[2]**staggered**   walked with great difficulty
[3]**peasants**   poor farmers or farm workers
[4]**San Carlos**   coastal town in eastern Spain
[5]**Ebro Delta**   an area of flat, rich land near the mouth of the Ebro River in eastern Spain

wondering how long it would be before we would see the enemy, and listening all the while for the first noises that would signal that ever mysterious event called contact,[6] and the old man still sat there.

"What animals were they?" I asked.

"There were three animals altogether," he explained. "There were two goats and a cat and then there were four pairs of pigeons."

"And you had to leave them?" I asked.

"Yes. Because of the artillery.[7] The captain told me to go because of the artillery."

"And you have no family?" I asked, watching the far end of the bridge where a few last carts were hurrying down the slope of the bank.

"No," he said, "only the animals I stated. The cat, of course, will be all right. A cat can look out for itself, but I cannot think what will become of the others."

"What politics have you?[8]" I asked.

"I am without politics," he said. "I am seventy-six years old. I have come twelve kilometers now and I think now I can go no further."

"This is not a good place to stop," I said. "If you can make it, there are trucks up the road where it forks for Tortosa."

"I will wait a while," he said, "and then I will go. Where do the trucks go?"

"Towards Barcelona," I told him.

"I know no one in that direction," he said. "But thank you very much. Thank you again very much."

He looked at me very blankly and tiredly, then said, having to share his worry with some one, "The cat will be all right, I am sure. There is no need to be unquiet about the cat. But the others. Now what do you think about the others?"

"Why they'll probably come through it all right."

"You think so?"

"Why not?" I said, watching the far bank where now there were no carts.

"But what will they do under the artillery when I was told to leave because of the artillery?"

"Did you leave the dove[9] cage unlocked?" I asked.

"Yes."

Then they'll fly."

"Yes, certainly they'll fly. But the others. It's better not to think about the others," he said.

"If you are rested I would go," I urged. "Get up and try to walk now."

"Thank you," he said and got to his feet, swayed from side to side and then sat down backwards in the dust.

"I was taking care of animals," he said dully, but no longer to me. "I was only taking care of animals."

There was nothing to do about him. It was Easter Sunday[10] and the Fascists[11] were advancing toward the Ebro. It was a gray overcast day with a low ceiling[12] so their planes were not up.

That and the fact that cats know how to look after themselves was all the good luck that old man would ever have.

[6]**artillery**	large, heavy guns
[7]**contact**	in war, the first exchange of fire
[8]**What politics have you?**	What political system do you believe in?
[9]**dove**	a family of birds, including pigeons; also a symbol for peace
[10]**Easter Sunday**	a Christian holiday that celebrates renewal of life
[11]**Fascists**	in Europe during the 1930's and 1940's, any political group that supported a right wing military dictatorship
[12]**a low ceiling**	cloudy conditions that make it difficult for airplane pilots to see the ground

5. Locate

On your own. Find the places in the story on this map of eastern Spain.

6. Retell

Pairwork. Divide the story into two parts. Then take turns retelling each part. Discuss these questions with your partner.

What change did the old man have to face?

What did he worry about most?

Why didn't he want to go to Barcelona?

What did he do in the end?

7. Interpret

a. Pairwork. Read the whole story again. Then look at the lines of dialogue on the left side of the chart on the next page. Read what each character said on the left, then write what you think the character was *really* thinking. You might want to write more than one possible thought for each line of dialogue.

"Where do you come from?"

"You'd better hurry... it's too dangerous to stay here."

What they said	What they were thinking
Narrator: Where do you come from?	*You'd better hurry...*
Old Man: From San Carlos. I was taking care of animals.	
Narrator: Oh.	
Narrator: This is not a good place to stop.	
Old Man: I will wait a while, and then I will go.	
Narrator: If you are rested I would go. Get up and try to walk now.	
Old Man: I was taking care of animals. I was only taking care of animals.	

b. Get together with another pair. Compare the right side of your charts and discuss any differences. If you wish, add ideas from your classmates to your own chart.

c. In the same group, prepare to present one set of your "What they were thinking" ideas to the rest of the class. Follow these steps.

1. Decide on two members of the group to role play the conversation between the old man and the narrator. These two characters should sit on chairs facing each other and read lines from the left side of the chart. Be sure to pause after each line.

2. The other two members will stand behind the main characters and read the "What they were thinking" lines aloud.

3. Rehearse your presentation two or three times before presenting it to the class.

d. Classwork. Discuss what you think might happen to the bridge, the old man, and the animals in the story. Offer some ideas and listen to those of your classmates. Then write down your own ideas.

8. Share Ideas

Groupwork. What did the narrator do when the old man decided not to move on? Was it the right thing to do? What would you have done? Choose the action you would have taken. Explain your choice to the group.

I would have...

a. left the old man alone

b. forced the old man to move across the bridge

c. helped the old man go back to get the goats

d. waited for the old man to rest, then tried to persuade him again

e. (your own idea) _____

Language Focus

Past Conjecture

I would have tried harder.

---

9. Journal Writing

a. On your own. How did you feel about the two characters in the story? What do you think the author feels? Support your opinions by referring to parts of the story.

b. How did you like the story? Explain your reaction.

Chapter 3: Transitions

*M*any cultures have special ceremonies that mark the change between childhood and adulthood. These "coming of age" ceremonies form a kind of bridge, over which young people must pass to become adult members of their community. Do you think these bridges are important and necessary?

◆ **1.** **Explore**

a. Classwork. Look at the examples of coming of age ceremonies in different cultures throughout this unit. About how old are the young people? What are they doing? How do you think they feel? Share ideas and experiences with your classmates.

b. Groupwork. Describe what happens in a typical coming of age ceremony in your culture or another one you know about. Here are some questions to think about.

How do people dress?

Who performs the ceremony?

What does the young person have to do?

How do people celebrate?

What kinds of food do they eat?

2. Journal Writing

On your own. Write about a ceremony or party you have had. It can be your own coming of age ceremony or any other important moment that marked a change in your life. Describe what happened and how you felt.

3. Listen

Classwork. You are going to hear about coming of age in the United States. Listen first for the main ideas. Then look at the web diagram. What information is missing? Listen again and fill in the missing information.

a. Pairwork. Take turns explaining part of the web diagram to your partner.

Study Strategy:

Listening for Specific Information

See page 164.

Study Strategy:

Making a Web Diagram

See page 166.

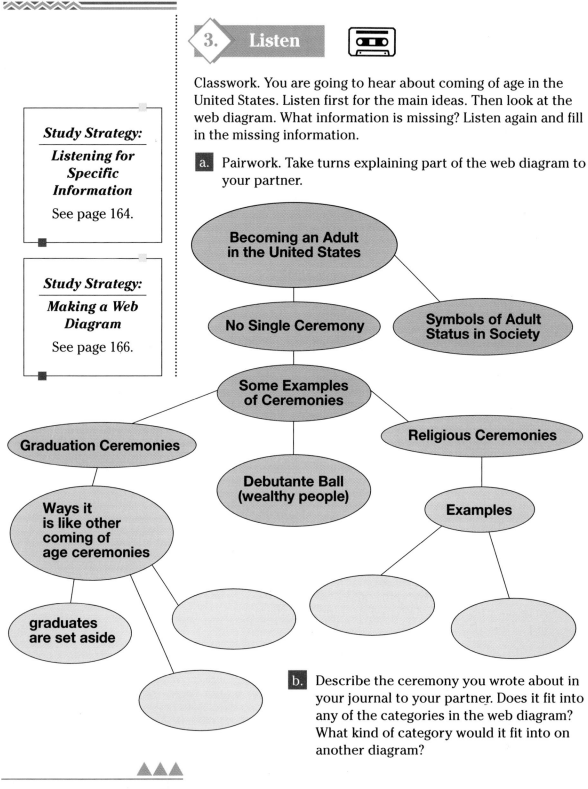

b. Describe the ceremony you wrote about in your journal to your partner. Does it fit into any of the categories in the web diagram? What kind of category would it fit into on another diagram?

4. **Shared Reading**

As you read this article, think about how the author feels as she writes about coming of age in her culture. Whose personal experience does she use as an example?

"I Felt Like a Queen"
by Suzanne Flores

Can you imagine planning your next birthday party for almost a year in advance, then, when your birthday arrives, wearing a long gown, dancing all night to a live orchestra,[1] and celebrating for two days? Many Mexican girls do just that on their fifteenth birthday, their *quince años.*[2]

An invitation to a *quince años* is an honor; it means not only getting all dressed up and having a great time, but also taking part in a ceremony that welcomes a girl into the adult world. In a way, it might be compared to the "coming out" party that some families have in the United States. Here, only rather rich "society" people have such parties, but in Mexico, both rich and poor families might have a *quince años*, hoping that it will improve the girl's chances of making an advantageous marriage.[3] A Mexican family might have to spend as much for this birthday as for a girl's wedding. If the family cannot afford it, they ask for help from godmothers and godfathers.[4] For instance, if you are asked to be the cake godmother, you bring the cake. When a Mexican *señorita* descends the stairs to the strains of *"Las Mañanitas"* and the flash of camera bulbs, then dances the "Blue Danube" with her father, there is no doubt she has come of age. From now on, she will change from a young girl in knee socks and braids to a young woman in high heels and make-up, and more than just her clothes will be different: The way she is treated will change, too. People will no longer see her as a little

---

[1]**live orchestra**   a real orchestra present at the party, not recorded beforehand

[2]***quince años***   fifteenth birthday, also called *quincenera*

[3]**an advantageous marriage**   a marriage that will improve one's social and economic position

[4]**godmother and godfather**   special adults in a child's life; sponsors at a Christian baptism

girl who can play games and help with the chores but as a person getting ready to become a wife and mother who will soon have adult responsibilities. This party recognizes that important step in life.

The *quince años* party happens mostly in smaller cities and towns, where tradition remains strong. It is part of the traditional view that a girl, in contrast to a boy, will not go to college or have a job but will soon marry and have children. This is her "graduation" ceremony—it says that she is ready to start dating and looking for a husband.

My Mexican mother-in-law still vividly[5] remembers her *quince años*, although it happened many years ago:

[5]**vividly**   in full detail

"Shortly after my fourteenth birthday, everyone began asking if we were going to have a *quince años*. Of course we were! We began by looking at gown patterns for me and all my cousins, right down to the youngest, since we all wanted to dress up. Everyone loved the planning and the excitement that began to build as we set the date for the Mass[6] at church, saw the seamstress, searched for our gentlemen dancing partners, and rehearsed the waltz with them. We did not rent a ballroom but decided to have the party in the patio of my house. The neighbors all helped to clean and decorate it, knowing that this party was for everyone.

"Finally, it was the morning of my birthday, bringing with it the first surprise of the day. Imagine waking up to live orchestra music and being the center of everyone's attention: I felt like a queen surrounded by all her subjects.[7] My uncle played in an orchestra and brought eight of his friends to serenade me with the Mexican birthday song, "*Las Mañanitas.*" Then my parents fed everyone a breakfast of *atole* (a thick, puddinglike drink) and *tamales* (steamed corn bread with a filling of either fruit or spicy meat).

"At noon we all went to church for the Mass of thanks and a beautiful speech by the *padre*[8] about how my parents felt seeing me pass from girlhood to this age so full of hopes and dreams. Then everyone was hugging me, and we were off to the photographer. Back home, I was surrounded by family, friends, and presents. We had more food—consomme,[9] rice, chicken *mole* (a spicy sauce of at least twelve ingredients, including nuts, chilies, chocolate, and spices), *tamales*, and drinks—and then the party began in earnest.[10]

"My father led me out for the first waltz. I danced all night, and the next day the party continued, with big chunks of birthday cake and more surprises in the celebration of my *quince años*. The young man who was my partner for the second dance later became my husband."

from *Faces* Magazine, February, 1988

[6]**Mass**   in the Catholic church, the main religious ceremony
[7]**subjects**   people ruled by a king or queen
[8]***padre***   Catholic religious leader; priest
[9]**consomme**   a clear soup; broth of meat or vegetables
[10]**in earnest** in a serious way

5. Share Ideas

Groupwork. Share ideas about the reading with your classmates. Here are some questions you might think about.

a. What is the purpose of the quince años in Mexican society? Do you think it is important or necessary?

b. How do poor families manage to give their daughters a quince años?

c. Why do you think the quince años happens mostly in smaller cities and towns?

d. Which part of the ceremony do you like best? Which part do you like least? Explain why.

6. Evaluate

a. Pairwork. Read this quotation from the story. What is your personal reaction to this traditional view? Discuss your opinion with your partner.

"It is part of the traditional view that a girl, in contrast to a boy, will not go to college or have a job but will soon marry and have children. This is her 'graduation' ceremony—it says that she is ready to start dating and looking for a husband."

b. Compare the traditional view expressed in the quotation with the modern view. Write your ideas in a chart like this.

Traditional View	Modern View
Girls will not go to college.	
Girls will not get jobs.	
Women are mainly wives and mothers.	

c. Discuss the advantages and disadvantages of both views.

7. Research

a. Pairwork. Find out what older people remember about a traditional coming of age ceremony. Follow these steps:

1. Arrange to interview a relative or older person in your community. Set up a special time and place for the interview.

2. Prepare your questions in advance. Try to find out as many details as you can about the older person's experience.

3. Prepare to take notes or tape record your interview.

4. Write a report based on your interview. Summarize the answers to your questions, and use quotes from the interview to make it interesting. Conclude your report by describing what it was like to interview this person. What did you learn? How did the person feel about it?

b. Classwork. Put your reports together. Add drawings, postcards, or copies of photographs if you can. Publish a class collection of "coming of age" ceremonies in different times and places. For more information about publishing a collection of writing, refer to the Writer's Guide on page 174.

Chapter 4: Life Spans

*T*he span of a bridge is the distance from one side to another. A person's life span is the length of time between birth and death. Relationships between friends and relatives are a lot like bridges. In this chapter, you will read about some of the ways people build new bridges or repair old ones in order to stay connected to the past, the future, and to one another.

1. List

a. Pairwork. What qualities do you think are important in a friend? State each quality two ways.

Example: I think it's important for a friend to be honest.
Honesty is an important quality.

List as many qualities as you can:

Our list of important qualities: ____*honesty*____ , _____ ,

_____ , _____ , _____

Language Focus:

Forming Adjectives from Nouns

generosity—
generous
honesty—
honest
importance—
important

---

b. Get together with another pair. Compare your lists. See if you want to add any more qualitities to your list.

2. Journal Writing

On your own. Choose the one quality from the list you made that you personally feel is *most* important. Write about it in your journal. Give an example situtation in which this quality is important.

3. Define

Groupwork. Suggest ways of finishing these sentences. Make as many different sentences as you can. Share your group's sentences with the class.

Friendship is knowing that _____

An example of friendship is when _____

Classwork. Read this song aloud.

YOU'VE GOT A FRIEND

by Carole King

When you're down, and troubled
And you need some love and care
And nothin', nothin' is going right
Close your eyes and think of me
And soon I will be there to
Brighten up even your darkest night.

You just call out my name
And you know wherever I am
I'll come runnin' to see you again.
Winter, spring, summer, or fall,
All you have to do is call
And I'll be there. You've got a friend.

If the sky above you
Grows dark and full of clouds
And that ol' north wind begins to blow
Keep your head together
And call my name out loud,
Soon you'll hear me knockin' at your door

You just call out my name
And you know wherever I am
I'll come runnin' to see you again.
Winter, spring, summer, or fall,
All you have to do is call
And I'll be there, yes, I will

Now, ain't[1] it good to know that you've got a friend
When people can be so cold?
They'll hurt you, yes, and desert[2] you
And take your soul if you let them
Oh, but don't you let them.

You just call out my name
And you know, wherever I am
I'll come runnin' to see you again.
Winter, spring, summer, or fall,
All you have to do is call
And I'll be there, yes, I will
You've got a friend. You've got a friend.
Ain't it good to know you've got a friend?

[1]**ain't** isn't it, in nonstandard English
[2]**desert** abandon, leave cruelly

Carole King (1942-   )

Carole King was born in New York City, and began to play the piano at the age of four. As a teenager, she liked to hang out at rock and roll concerts, and started a group of her own. At Queens College, she met Gerry Coffin, with whom she began to write songs and who later became her husband. Together, they wrote some of the most popular songs of the 1960's and 1970's, including "Locomotion," "Will You Still Love Me Tomorrow," and "Up On The Roof."

5. **Share Ideas**

Classwork. Discuss your reactions to the song with your classmates. Here are some other questions to think about.

a. Does it fit your personal definition of friendship?

b. According to the song, when do friends need each other most?

c. How can a friend "brighten up even your darkest night"?

 6. **Role Play**

Pairwork. Imagine a situation when "nothing is going right." Write out a dialogue in which one friend calls another to ask for help. What would a good friend say or do? Practice your dialogue, then perform it for the class.

 **7.** **Share a Poem**

This poem was originally written in Spanish by a poet from Nicaragua, Daisy Zamora. Listen to the Spanish version first. Then read the English translation.

Daisy Zamora (1950-   )

Daisy Zamora was born in Managua, Nicaragua in 1950. As a young girl, she attended private religious schools and was later trained as a psychologist. However, she is best known as a poet and a painter. She was also active in the political movement that overthrew the dictator Somoza Bebayle in 1979. She now lives with her husband and three children in Managua, where she also teaches and continues to write poetry.

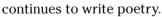

Letter to My Sister Who Lives in a Foreign Land

by Daisy Zamora
tr. Margaret Randall & Elinor Randall

. . . And I was sent south of the village of Wei
—covered with little laurel arbors—
and you to the north of Roku-hoku,
until all we had in common were thoughts
and memories

> *—"Letter from the Exiled One,"–Li-Tai-Po*

I still remember our first games:
parades and paper dolls,
and Teresa, the doll we couldn't stand:
Teresa-are-you-able-to-come-and-set-the-table.

Life doesn't move backwards and I want to know you.
Re-know you.
That is, know you all over again.
Of course there will be things I'll recognize.
I'm interested in your special places,
your friends, so different from mine
who speak another language and follow other paths.

Danbury, Hamden, and Middletown,
Hartford and Meriden. All those places
so familiar to you and to your memory.
In our shared blood I have lived two lives,
many lives.

 8. **Match**

On your own. Find these people, places, and things
in the poem.

a. a Chinese poet

b. the title of a Chinese poem

c. two villages in China

d. a doll

e. five towns in North America

9. Share Ideas

Groupwork. What kind of bridge does the poet want to build? Why is it important to her? Share your ideas with the group.

10. Write

a. On your own. Write a letter, note, or poem to a relative or friend who does not live nearby. Remind the person of a memory you both share. Write it in the language you would naturally use to communicate with this person.

b. Groupwork. Share your letter with a small group of classmates. Read it first in the original, then explain it to the group in English.

11. Preview

a. Classwork. Look at the title of the article before you begin to read. What do you think the article is about? Look at the photograph. What kinds of bridges are the people in this picture building?

b. Pairwork. What words come to mind when you think of an older person? Make a list of descriptive words. Which words describe positive qualities? Which describe negative ones? Group your words on a chart like this one.

Positive (+)	Negative (−)	Neutral (neither + nor −)

Across Ages
by Scott Brodeur

What words come to mind when you think of an older person?

If your answers are: mean, cranky[1], helpless, or boring, you are not alone. They are the same words some Philadelphia[2] students used to describe older people.

That was before the students joined Across Ages, a new program. Across Ages pairs youths with older people who act as their mentors.[3] The purpose is to get teenagers and older people to understand and help one another.

"When we first found out we were going to have mentors, we asked how old they would be," says Will Bush. "They told us 40 and older. We thought, man, that's old."

"But when the first meeting was over, nobody wanted the mentors to leave. We were having so much fun."

Mentors meet with students once a week. Together, they talk about school, homework, personal problems, or whatever else comes up. They also go on trips to places like basketball games, museums, and restaurants.

A New Start

Reaching out to someone older has helped Steven Mason find direction in his life. Before Across Ages, he was missing school. He wasn't doing his homework. He didn't have a lot of faith in himself.

Then Steven met his mentor, Earl P. Powell. Now he's getting A's and B's instead of failing.

"When we get together, we go eat somewhere and talk, " says Steven. "We talk about my grades and what I want to be when I grow up. Mr. Powell encourages me to do my best in school. He makes sure I do my homework. He really cares."

Some students have problems at home. Many live with just one parent. Others are exposed to[4] violent crimes as well as drugs and alcohol at a young age. They like the extra attention they get from their mentors.

"When our mentors talk to us, they listen and understand," says Will. Mentors are often easier to talk to than parents or relatives, he says.

[1]**cranky**	easily annoyed or angered
[2]**Philadelphia**	the largest city in Pennsylvania
[3]**mentors**	wise and trusted teachers or counselors
[4]**are exposed to**	come into contact with; forced to see

"Parents are busy people. Sometimes, they can be too busy to hear everything a child has to say," says Anna Mizell, 68. "But I'm retired. I have plenty of time to listen and help."

Antonio Walker is glad for that.

"Mentors give great advice," he says.

"You can trust them because they have all this experience. They know how it is."

Sam Wyche, 75, is the mentor for Will and Antonio. Sam says he gets as much out of the program as the students.

"I enjoy the kids. I like doing things with them," Sam says. "They're interested in what I have to tell them. That makes me feel good."

Sam got involved for another reason, too. "I hope I'm helping kids who really need it," Sam says. "I wasn't the greatest boy in the world when I was their age. But it's even tougher to grow up now, and I want to help push these kids through it.[5]"

Pat Lewis, 62, agrees with Sam.

"Children can't be children today," Pat says. "There are pressures to get into drugs and to have sex at an early age. It's not even safe for many kids to walk outside after dark anymore."

Pat often tells stories about safer times when she was a kid. Students love to hear her talk about trolley[6] rides and old-fashioned cars.

"You can learn from the stories," says Aaron Taggart, "They're fun to hear."

Pat also encourages students to try new things and to build on their talents.[7] Together, they've worked on arts, crafts, and writing projects.

"So many students are talented," Pat says. "Our job as mentor is to find those talents and to urge them to keep at it."

Joy Harris loves showing Pat her poems. Pat's poems have been published in books. Joy has been writing since she was 7.

"Mrs. Lewis will be on the other side of the room and stop everything when she sees me," Joy says. "It's great to have someone who takes an interest in my work like she does."

But Pat does more than just read Joy's poems. "She tells me my poems are good," Joy says. "She says I have to keep doing it because I have a special talent. I smiled when she said that. It made me feel really great."

A Special Project

One project that helped mentors and students learn about each other was an oral history. Students interviewed the mentors and recorded what the mentors shared about their lives.

Through the oral histories and spending time together, students began to realize something: Older people are regular people too. Even some myths students used to believe are disappearing.

"I used to think older people got tired quickly," says Antonio. "But when Mr. Powell plays basketball with us, and we're dragging tired, he's like, 'Come on, just another couple shots.' "

Finding your own mentor can be helpful to students everywhere, Steven says. "I would tell other kids to find an older person who can be their mentor," he says. "It's fun. And it's great to always have someone there for you."

Steven and the other students have changed since they started in Across Ages. When you ask them to describe older people, the words they use now are: nice, fun, caring, and funny.

"I never thought I'd tell someone I had a friend who was 75 years old," says Antonio. "But now I do."

[5]**push these kids through it**   help them succeed
[6]**trolley**   an electric streetcar
[7]**talents**   natural abilities or skills

13. Share Ideas

Groupwork. Discuss the article with the members of your group. Here are some questions to think about.

a. How did the young people in this article change?

b. What did the younger people learn from the older people?

c. What did the older people learn from the younger people?

d. Would you agree to participate in a program like "Across Ages"? Why or why not?

14. Write

On your own. Think about the readings and discussions of friendship you have had. Look at the sentences you wrote with your group in #3. Write a longer explanation of what friendship means to you. Write at least one complete paragraph.

Begin by organizing your ideas in the form of a cluster like the one below. You can add to this one or make a completely different cluster of your own.

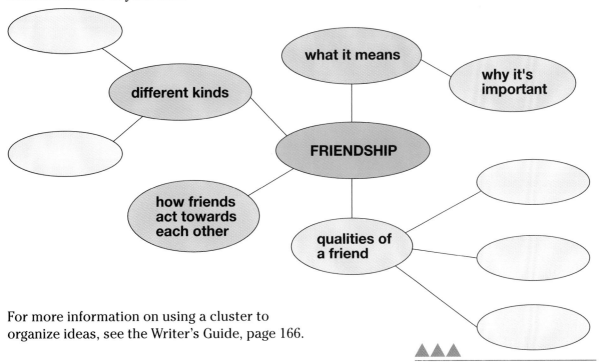

For more information on using a cluster to organize ideas, see the Writer's Guide, page 166.

Chapter 5: Bridges Across Time and Space

*S*cience fiction writers build bridges by imagining what life will be like in the future. In this chapter, you will read a selection from *The Martian Chronicles,* in which science fiction writer Ray Bradbury invites readers to look at one vision of the future. How can this kind of imaginary bridge help people build a better world?

Study Strategy:

Taking Notes in a Chart

See page 169.

1. **Research**

Pairwork. Search in an encyclopedia or science dictionary. Find the following facts about Earth and Mars.

	Earth	Mars
Distance from the sun		
Length of year		
Number of moons		
Average atmospheric temperature		
Composition of atmosphere (gases)		
Signs of life		

2. Preview

a. Classwork. Based on what you know about Mars, do you think life could exist there? Share your ideas with your classmates.

b. Groupwork. Imagine intelligent life on Mars or on another planet. Discuss how the alien creatures might look, act, and communicate with outsiders. Make a sketch of your aliens and describe them to the class.

c. On your own. Read this description of *The Martian Chronicles*, a science fiction novel written by Ray Bradbury and first published in 1946.

This is the story of the people who, as the first arrivals in a far-off land, failed in their efforts to build a new world in the image of the world they had left. It also tells of a strange, dying race—men and women with eyes like golden coins who wore masks to hide their feelings and could stroke books to bring forth songs.

This is a brilliant and imaginative fantasy that is deeply rooted in reality. It is a prophecy that is made without despair.

This is the work of one of America's finest storytellers. To read Ray Bradbury is to escape in time and space to that world where fancy and irony show people things about themselves they would otherwise fail to see.

d. Classwork. From this description, would you be interested in reading the novel? Why or why not? Explain to your classmates.

> ### 3. Read
>
> On your own. Read this selection from *The Martian Chronicles*.
> As you read, try to imagine yourself in the position of the
> colonist from Earth, Tomas Gomez. How would you feel? What
> would you do?

August 2002: Night Meeting

It was a long road going into darkness and hills and he
held to the wheel, now and again reaching into his lunch
bucket and taking out a piece of candy. He had been driving
steadily for an hour, with no other car on the road, no light, just
the road going under, the hum, the roar, and Mars out there, so
quiet. Mars was always quiet, but quieter tonight than any
other. The deserts and empty seas swung by him, and the
mountains against the stars.

There was smell of Time in the air tonight. He smiled and
turned the fancy[1] in his mind. There was a thought. What did
Time smell like? Like dust and clocks and people. And if you
wondered what Time sounded like it sounded like water
running in a dark cave and voices crying and dirt dropping
down upon hollow box lids, and rain. And, going further, what
did Time look like? Time looked like snow dropping silently into
a black room or it looked like a silent film in an ancient theater,
one hundred billion faces falling like those New Year balloons,
down and down into nothing. And that was how Time smelled
and looked and sounded. And tonight—Tomas shoved a hand
into the wind outside the truck—tonight you could almost touch
Time.

He drove the truck between hills of Time. His neck prickled[2]
and he sat up, watching ahead.

He pulled into a little dead Martian town, stopped the
engine, and let the silence come in around him. He sat, not
breathing, looking out at the white buildings in the moonlight.
Uninhabited for centuries. Perfect, faultless, in ruins, yes, but
perfect, nevertheless.

---

[1]**fancy**   an interesting or amusing thought
[2]**prickled**   felt a tingling sensation

He started the engine and drove on another mile or more before stopping again, climbing out, carrying his lunch bucket, and walking to a little promontory[3] where he could look back at that dusty city. He felt very good, very much at peace.

Perhaps five minutes later there was a sound. Off in the hills, where the ancient highway curved, there was a motion, a dim light, and then a murmur.[4]

Tomas turned slowly with the coffee cup in his hand.

And out of the hills came a strange thing.

It was a machine like a jade-green insect, a praying mantis,[5] delicately rushing through the cold air, indistinct,[6] countless green diamonds winding over its body, and red jewels that glittered[7] with multifaceted[8] eyes. Its six legs fell upon the ancient highway with the sounds of a sparse rain which dwindled[9] away, and from the back of the machine a Martian with melted gold for eyes looked down at Tomas as if he were looking into a well.

Tomas raised his hand and thought Hello! automatically but did not move his lips, for this *was* a Martian. But Tomas had swum in blue rivers on Earth, with strangers passing on the road, and eaten in strange houses with strange people, and his weapon had always been his smile. He did not carry a gun. And he did not feel the need of one now, even with the little fear that gathered about his heart at this moment.

The Martian's hands were empty too. For a moment they looked across the cool air at each other.

It was Tomas who moved first.

"Hello!" he called.

"Hello!" called the Martian in his own language.

They did not understand each other.

"Did you say hello?" they both asked.

---

[3] **promontory** a high ridge of land
[4] **murmur** a low, continuous sound
[5] **praying mantis** a large pale green insect with forelimbs often held in a praying position
[6] **indistinct** not clear
[7] **glittered** shone
[8] **multifaceted** having many parts
[9] **dwindled** slowly disappeared

"What did you say?" they said, each in a different tongue. They scowled.[10]

"Who are you?" said Tomas in English.

"What are you doing here?" In Martian; the stranger's lips moved.

"Where are you going?" they said, and looked bewildered.[11]

"I'm Tomas Gomez."

"I'm Muhe Ca."

Neither understood, but they tapped their chests with the words and then it became clear.

And then the Martian laughed. "Wait!" Tomas felt his head touched, but no hand had touched him. "There!" said the Martian in English. "That is better!"

"You learned my language, so quick!"

"Nothing at all."

They looked, embarrassed with a new silence, at the steaming coffee he had in one hand.

"Something different?" said the Martian, eyeing him and the coffee, referring to them both, perhaps.

"May I offer you a drink?" said Tomas.

"Please."

The Martian slid down from his machine.

---

[10]**scowled**   frowned angrily
[11]**bewildered**   puzzled

Ray Bradbury (1920-   )

Ray Bradbury was born in 1920 in Waukegan, Illinois. He published his first story for a science fiction magazine in 1940. *The Martian Chronicles* was his second and most well known book. It was produced as a movie in 1960 and as a television miniseries in 1980. His other works of fantasy and science fiction include *The Illustrated Man* and *Fahrenheit 451*, which were also made into motion pictures.

▲▲▲

4. Role Play

Pairwork. Act out the conversation between Tomas and the Martian. Remember, one of you will have to speak in a language other than English for part of the conversation.

5. Share Ideas

Groupwork. What's your reaction to the story? Share ideas with the people in your group. Here are some questions to think about.

a. Which part of the story was most interesting?

b. Is it similar to any story you have read or heard before? Please explain.

c. How did you feel after you finished this selection?

d. Most science fiction stories teach readers a lesson. What lesson do you think Ray Bradbury wanted to get across in this part of the novel?

e. Do you want to read more of *The Martian Chronicles*? Why or why not?

6. Analyze

On your own. Reread the second paragraph in the selection. How does the author describe "time"? Group the words and phrases used to describe "time" into three categories:

TIME		
Smells like . . .	Sounds like . . .	Looks like . . .
dust		

Language Focus:

Describe

*Describing
Perceptions*

▪ What did "time"
look like to
Tomas?

▪ It looked like
snow . . . .

7. Describe

a. Pairwork. Choose another concept or emotion you can describe in a similar way, such as peace, success, joy, or fear. How does it smell? How does it sound? How does it look? Use your imagination to think of as many descriptive words and phrases as you can.

b. Look over the list of words with your partner. Use some of these words to write a short poem.

8. Apply

Pairwork. Imagine that you have been asked to collect things to place in a time capsule from your city or town that will not be opened for 1000 years. The capsule will be carefully sealed so that nothing inside will age or be destroyed. What do you want the people of the future to know about the way you live? Make a list of the things you would put into the capsule. Here are some ideas for things to include.

> newspaper articles
>
> clothing items
>
> photos

Get together with another pair and exchange lists.
Give reasons for your choices.

9. Write

Groupwork. Reflect on the story. How would you like to be able to learn another language so quickly? Think about some other things that might be possible in the future. Work with your group to write a description of an ideal society. Here are some ideas to help you get started.

1. In *The Martian Chronicles*, Ray Bradbury wrote about a group of people who wanted to leave the problems of Earth behind and create a new society on Mars. Suppose you had a chance to build a new society on a different planet. What would it be like? How would it be different from life on Earth? Discuss your ideas with your group.

2. Choose one of these aspects of life in your ideal society to write about. Each member of the group should choose a different topic.

    housing

    transportation

    food

    money

    social life

3. Make a list of your ideas on paper. Discuss them with your classmates before you begin to write.

4. Write a paragraph about your topic. Read it aloud to the group. Ask someone in the group to tell you the main ideas.

5. Ask for suggestions from the group on how to make your paragraph better. See the Writer's Guide (p. 174) for more ideas on revising your first draft.

6. With your group, decide on the best order for putting the paragraphs together. Prepare a presentation of your group's work for the rest of the class.

Activity Menu

1. Construct a Flat Beam

Place two large hardcover books on their ends, about eight inches apart. What do you predict will happen if you attempt to span the distance with a flat piece of paper? Fold a sheet of 8.5 × 11 inch paper lengthwise every inch or so, making each crease in the opposite direction.

Do you predict that the folded paper will make a stronger or weaker beam? Tell a classmate. Place the folded paper between the two books. Place a paper clip, a coin, and finally a small book on the beam. How much weight will it take? Was your prediction correct?

2. Research a Bridge

Find out as much as you can about a bridge in your city or state or a well-known bridge somewhere else. Find when and why it was built. What kind of bridge is it? What materials were used in it? Is it a bridge for automobiles? for people? for railroad trains? How much is it used? How was it paid for? Use an encyclopedia or books and magazines from the library to help you find facts about your bridge.

Take notes and write a report on your bridge or tell the rest of the class about it.

3. Request Support

During the administration of Franklin D. Roosevelt (1933–1945), a great many bridges, roads, and public buildings were constructed under a special U.S. government program called the Works Progress Administration. This program helped people who were unemployed, and it produced some of the country's finest architecture. The Golden Gate Bridge in San Francisco, for example, was built during this period.

Write a letter to your Senator or Congressman, proposing funding for a construction project in your area. Explain why your community needs this project.

Describe the benefits both present and future and speculate on what might happen if it is not funded.

4. Analyze a Popular Song

Select a popular song about love or friendship. Listen carefully to the words several times. What kind of relationship is it about? What does it say about life? Tell a classmate.

5. Plan a Ceremony

Work with a small group of classmates to plan a ceremony that will mark a transition. For example, it could mark the completion of the course or the end of school year. Decide who you will invite, what will happen during the ceremony, what you will wear, and how you will celebrate. Present your plan to the rest of the class.

6. Write a Poem

Write a poem to someone with whom you have a close relationship. The poem can be long or short, but it should form a "bridge" between you and the person to whom it is addressed. Share your poem with a classmate.

7. Search for an Ideal Mentor

What would you look for in a mentor? What kind of experience and background would your ideal person have? Write a "volunteer opportunity" notice that specifies these qualifications and abilities. Describe special ways you would like a mentor to help you.

8. Communicate Friendship

How can former enemies become friends again? Think of some symbols people use to communicate that they no longer wish to fight. Imagine a situation in which two people are so angry that they refuse to speak to each other. Suggest a way one of them can send a signal to the other that would help end the conflict. Try acting out your situation with a classmate.

The Eighth Wonder of the World

The Brooklyn Bridge is considered[1] one of the greatest engineering feats of the 19th century. For many years after its completion in 1883, it was the longest suspension bridge in the world, and the first to use steel cables. The bridge, which New Yorkers liked to call "the eighth wonder of the world," spans the East River between the boroughs[2] of Brooklyn and Manhattan in New York City.

The bridge was the master work of John Augustus Roebling, a German immigrant who unfortunately did not live to see its completion. Mr. Roebling died as a result of a construction accident in 1871, only two years after work on the bridge began. His son, Washington Roebling, took over as chief engineer, but soon became very ill from a disease caused by his work on the bridge.

Unable to move from his bed, Washington Roebling directed construction by watching from his apartment window. Several times a day, he sent messages with his wife, Emily Roebling, to and from the construction crews. In the process, Mrs. Roebling learned more and more about bridge construction, and soon began to take responsibility for many of the important decisions herself.

Today, the Brooklyn Bridge is still a vital link[3] in the city's transportation system, and is considered a work of great architectural beauty that has continued to inspire[4] numerous artists, poets, muscians, and writers.

[1] **considered**　thought of
[2] **borough**　part of a city or state
[3] **link**　part of a system
[4] **inspire**　to give creative energy

Poetry of Friendship

by José Marti　/　tr. by Raúl Nino

I cultivate a white rose
In June as in January
For a genuine friend,
That gives his unadorned hand

And for the cruelty that plucks
This heart that lives within
I do not cultivate gardenias nor weeds
I cultivate a white rose.

APPENDIX A
Guide to Study Strategies

 1. **Brainstorming**

Brainstorming is a good way to collect ideas for writing. It is an especially useful strategy to use with a partner or with a group of people.

To brainstorm a set of ideas, follow these steps :

- Write your topic on a piece of paper. This might be a word, a phrase, or a question.
- Think about your topic and write down every idea that comes to mind. Don't evaluate your ideas. Just think and write quickly.

Example:

Topic: **Important decisions**

> *when to get married*
> *where to live*
> *whether or not to go to college*
> *who to marry*

After brainstorming, reread your list and circle the ideas that interest you.

2. **Classifying**

Classifying means organizing information into groups or categories. For example, you might classify a list of clothing into two groups:

Example:

(unclassified information)

    coat, boots, bathing suit, sweater, shorts, T-shirt, parka, gloves

(classified information)

Cold Weather Clothing	Hot Weather Clothing
coat	bathing suit
boots	shorts
sweater	T-shirt
parka	
gloves	

3. **Listening for Specific Information**

Listening for specific information can help you listen carefully and understand what you hear. Before you listen to a lecture or a tape recording, ask yourself the questions below:

- What am I going to hear about? What is the topic?
- What do I already know about the topic?
- What questions do I have about the topic? What do I hope to learn?
- What kinds of information do I expect to hear? Dates? Names? Descriptions?

 4. **Making a Story Map**

Making a story map helps you focus on important information in a story. When you make a story map, look for these main parts of the story:

Characters:	Who are the people in the story?
Setting:	Where does the story take place?
The problem:	What is the central issue?
	What are the characters trying to do?
Important Events:	What happens in the story?

Title: _____

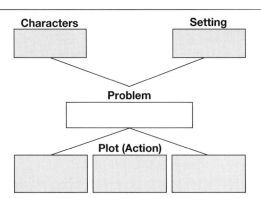

 5. **Making a Time Line**

Making a time line is a way to organize information visually. A time line helps you see the order of events over time. It can also help you find examples of cause and effect.

Example: **Time Line of Spacecraft Exploration**

1957	┼	First artificial Earth satellite First animal in space
1959	┼	First television images of the Earth from space
1961	┼	First human in space First human to orbit the Earth
1963	┼	First woman in space
1965	┼	First space walk
1966	┼	First spacecraft to enter the atmosphere of another planet (Venus) First spacecraft to orbit the Moon First successful soft landing on the Moon
1968	┼	First manned orbit of the Moon
1969	┼	First landing of humans on the Moon

6. ▷ Making a Tree Diagram

Making a tree diagram is a useful way to organize your ideas. Before you make a tree diagram, you might want to first list ideas about the topic. Then reread your list of ideas looking for ways to group your information. Write these categories or groups on your tree diagram. Then list ideas in each group.

Example:

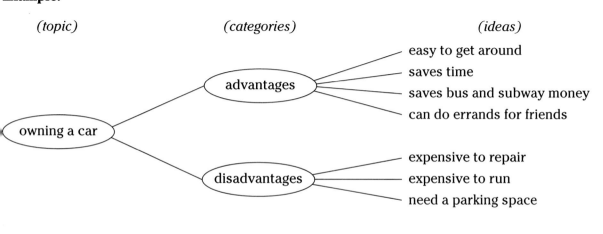

(topic)   *(categories)*   *(ideas)*

owning a car

advantages
- easy to get around
- saves time
- saves bus and subway money
- can do errands for friends

disadvantages
- expensive to repair
- expensive to run
- need a parking space

▲▲▲

7. Making a Web Diagram

Making a web diagram or a cluster diagram is a good way to collect ideas before you start to write. Making a web diagram can also help you see connections between big ideas and details.

Follow these steps to make a web diagram:

1. Write your topic in the center of a piece of paper. Circle it.

2. Think about your topic. What words and ideas come to mind? Write each thought in a smaller circle and connect it by a line to the circle in the center.

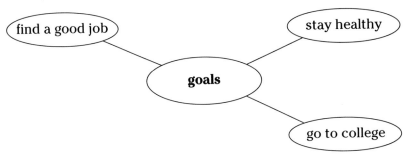

3. Think about the ideas in the smaller circles. What details come to mind? Write your ideas and connect them to the smaller circles.

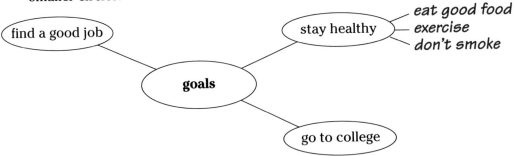

8. Predicting

What do you think will happen next in the story? What do you think the outcome will be? When you answer questions like these, you are predicting.

When you predict, you use what you already know about a topic, person, or event. Using what you already know helps you make a logical prediction. Making predictions helps you focus on the material you are studying. You make a prediction and then read to check if your prediction is correct.

9. Previewing

Previewing is a strategy that can help you understand what you read. The word *preview* means "to look before." To preview an article or story, look over the whole reading before you start to read.

- Look at the title and ask yourself questions about it. What does the title mean to you? What do you think the article or story is about?
- Look at any pictures and predict what the reading is about.
- Recall what you already know about the topic. Think of other things you would like to learn about the topic.
- Read the first paragraph and the last paragraph. Try to figure out the main idea of the reading.
- Set a purpose for reading. Decide what you hope to find out as you read.

10. Quickwriting

Quickwriting, or freewriting, is a useful way to collect ideas for writing. Follow these steps to quickwrite:

1. Choose a topic—something you want to write about.

2. For five to ten minutes, write quickly. Don't worry about grammar or spelling. If you can't think of a word in English, write it in your native language. The important thing is to write without stopping.

3. If you can't think of anything to write, put that down or write the same word over and over again.

4. When you have finished writing, read over your ideas. Circle the ideas that you might want to explore further.

Example:

> *What is a lake in a storm like? I live near a lake. When it's windy the waves get big, like the waves on the ocean. I can sometimes hear the waves from my house, like some big monster walking on the beach. What else can I say? What else can I say? Waves, waves, waves. What do waves smell like? What do they taste like? If a wave could talk, what would it say? Waves in a storm make me feel uncomfortable—not peaceful . . .*

11. Taking Notes in a Chart

Taking notes helps you organize and remember important information. When you take notes, write down the most important information only. To save time and space, write short phrases instead of sentences. The notes in the chart below were made after reading an article about the writer Nicholasa Mohr.

Example: **Nicholasa Mohr**

Paragraph	Topic	Details
2	family	<ul><li>parents from Puerto Rico</li><li>lived in New York City</li><li>7 children</li></ul>
3	career as an artist	<ul><li>studied at several art schools</li><li>exhibited her paintings</li><li>did pictures for book jackets</li></ul>
4	career as a writer	<ul><li>wrote novels and short stories</li><li>wrote about Puerto Rican immigrants</li><li>received an honorary Doctor of Letters degree</li></ul>

12. Using Context

Sometimes you can guess the meaning of an unfamiliar word by looking at the context—the other words in the sentence or nearby sentences. While you might not be able to figure out the exact meaning of the word, you may be able to determine its general meaning. This allows you to read without looking up every new word you meet. The examples below show some of the ways you can use context to guess the meaning of new words. The underlined words in the sentences provide context to help you guess the meaning of the boldfaced words.

A definition:

> The **period** of a wave means <u>the time it takes for succeeding waves to pass a fixed point.</u>

A description:

> Near the coast, the pattern of waves becomes more **orderly**—<u>a series of long, evenly spaced ridges.</u>

> Luis Herrera is a **frail** person, only <u>five feet, three inches tall and 115 pounds.</u>

A comparison or contrast:

> In New York, the family lived in a **cramped** apartment, very <u>different</u> from their <u>comfortable house</u> in Haiti.

> Luis Herrera was an **amateur** cyclist for four years, but when he turned sixteen, he became a <u>professional.</u>

A related series of words:

> Harriet Tubman was a <u>strong,</u> **determined** woman.

Cause and effect:

> I was so **absorbed** that <u>I didn't hear footsteps coming up behind me.</u>

Setting:

> While we were <u>on the ship,</u> <u>a wave crashed through</u> the large **hatch**; I got soaking wet and my wife, who was already <u>in bed,</u> was completely drenched.

A synonym:

> Thousands of slaves <u>ran away</u> each year. Some **fled** to get away from cruel owners.

APPENDIX B
Writer's Guide

The Writer's Guide is a series of suggestions that can help you work toward getting your ideas down on paper in finished form, ready for others to read. These suggestions are intended to guide you through some steps that work well for many writers. Use this guide as a menu. As you gain experience, you will learn to select and adapt the steps into a personal writing process that works best for you.

As you begin a writing assignment, start at the top of the diagram and move clockwise around the circle. Ask yourself questions as you go. Remember that the process is not fixed or rigid. Feel free to move back and forth between the steps whenever you need to recycle ideas or revise what you have written.

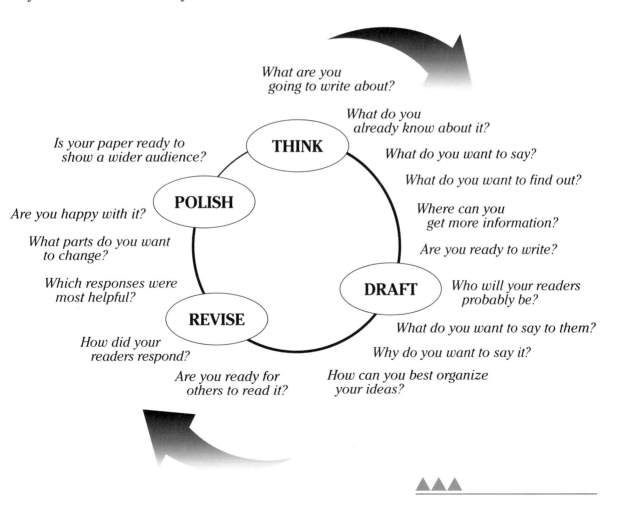

What are you going to write about?

What do you already know about it?

What do you want to say?

What do you want to find out?

Where can you get more information?

Are you ready to write?

THINK

Is your paper ready to show a wider audience?

POLISH

Are you happy with it?

What parts do you want to change?

Which responses were most helpful?

REVISE

How did your readers respond?

Are you ready for others to read it?

DRAFT

Who will your readers probably be?

What do you want to say to them?

Why do you want to say it?

How can you best organize your ideas?

1. Think

Reflect	Gather your thoughts about something that happened in the past or on a topic that you have strong feelings about. Take a walk or find a peaceful place where you can relax and concentrate.
Visualize	Paint a picture in your mind's eye of something that might happen in another place or time. Add as many details as you can.
Keep a Journal	Write down your thoughts and feelings as they happen, or as you think about a specific topic. Journal entries can be as long or as short as you wish, and in any style you choose. You can also use your journal to record some of the other activities listed below.
Quickwrite	Quickwriting is a great way to explore your own ideas and experiences related to a topic. Decide about how long you want to spend at it, then concentrate as hard as you can on the topic. Write whatever comes into your head, but don't stop thinking and writing until the time period is up. If you want to continue, take a break before you start again.
Discuss	Try out your ideas on a friend. Express your own opinion, but be sure to listen to others, too. The more you talk and listen, the clearer your own ideas will become.
Brainstorm	Work with a partner or a small group of classmates to think of ideas related to a topic. Think as hard as you can, then say aloud the words or phrases that come into your mind. One person in your pair or small group can write down the ideas. When the session is over, you can decide which ideas you think are important.
Make a List	Lists are especially useful when you are trying to think of a lot of examples of a category, like *walls built by people* or *qualities you look for in a friend*. Since two heads are better than one, it is a good idea to make lists with a friend whenever you can.
Do Research	Get more information about your topic by reading or asking other people. Think of some specific questions before you begin. Decide who you can ask or where you can look for the answers. Try checking out the library for books, newspapers, magazines, and encyclopedia articles related to your topic. Take notes on the important things you hear or read.
Focus Your Ideas	From all you have thought about, decide on the one main thing you want to say.

Organize Ideas   Think about ways of relating ideas to each other by making a chart or diagram. It doesn't have to be beautiful, as long as you can understand it and explain it to a classmate. Here are some examples of charts and diagrams used in this book.

Charts

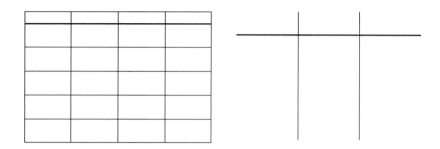

Diagrams

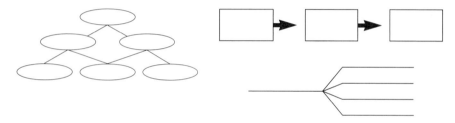

⬦ **2.** ⟩ **Write a First Draft**

Have a Purpose   Ask yourself why you are writing. Do you want to describe something or someone? Do you want to express your opinion or convince your reader that something is true? Whatever your purpose is, keep it clearly in mind as you begin to write.

Have a Plan   Look back over everything you have written down so far—lists, quickwriting, journal entries, and notes. You may want to jot down a short outline, or plan. You might also just decide to keep your plan in mind as you sit down to begin your first draft. What are you going to say? Where will you start? How will you finish? Use your plan as a map, to help you move toward your goal. Keep in mind, however, that it is all right to change the plan itself as you explore new directions and discover new ideas.

Have an Audience in Mind	Who do you expect to read what you write? Choose an audience, either real or imaginary, and keep this group of readers in mind as you write your first draft. Knowing who you are writing for helps you decide on the best ways of saying things. In most cases, your first audience will be your classmates and your teacher. However, you can pretend that your paper or letter will reach other readers (and maybe it really will!)
Get It Down on Paper	Just write! Don't worry about making mistakes. Try to get your ideas down on paper as completely as you can, but don't worry if you get stuck or if some parts seem too long. Keep asking yourself what else your readers might want to know. Stop writing your first draft when you are ready to show it to a small group of classmates and to your teacher.
Invite Responses	Ask your readers to respond to your first draft in one or more of these ways.

- Read your paper aloud. Ask your classmates or your teacher to tell you the most interesting parts. Ask them what else they would like to know.
- Make copies for your readers. Ask them to tell you what they think it is about. Ask yourself if your readers understood what you meant to say.
- Ask one of your classmates to read your paper aloud. Does it sound the way you thought it would? Do you want to change anything? Ask your classmates to show you parts where they were not sure what you meant

3. Revise

Think Again	Read your paper aloud. Ask yourself if there is anything more you want to say, or if there is anything you want to clarify.
Use Responses	Think about your classmates' and your teacher's responses. Which ones were most helpful? The decision to change your writing is yours, so be sure to use only the responses that *you* think will make your paragraph or paper better.
Reorganize	Ask yourself (or a classmate) if there is any better way to organize your ideas. You may want to revise your first plan or rework an earlier chart or diagram.

Write Again (and Again!)   Sit down and rewrite your paper until you are happy with it. Show it to your readers again. This time, ask for specific ways they feel your paper can be improved. Decide which of their ideas you want to include as you revise a second time.

4. Polish

Check Grammar   Are your sentences complete? Do your verbs agree with your subjects? Is your use of verb tenses consistent? Ask your teacher if you are not sure.

Check Spelling   Check a dictionary or use a spell check program to be sure your spelling is correct.

Check Punctuation   Proofread your paper to be sure all the periods, commas, and other punctuation marks are in the right places. Check with your teacher if you are not sure.

Check for Smooth Transitions   Read your finished piece aloud one more time. How does it sound? Does it flow smoothly from one idea to the next? Ask your teacher or a classmate for suggestions.

CREDITS

Illustrations — Martucci Studio
Photo Research — Susan Van Etten and
                    Martucci Studio

▲▲▲

ᲒEXT PERMISSIONS

2 "The Waves of Matsuyama" from *Poems of a Mountain Home* by Saigyo, translated by Burton Watson. Copyright © 1991 by Columbia University Press. Reprinted by permission of the publisher.

8 From *The Sea Around Us* by Rachel Carson. Copyright © 1951 by Rachel Carson. Reprinted by permission of Oxford University Press.

20 "Waves of Immigrants" graph from *The Los Angeles Times,* November 11, 1993. Copyright © 1993 by the Los Angeles Times Syndicate. Reprinted by permission.

23 "I was born . . ." by Saverio Rizzo from *The Immigrants Speak: Italian Immigrants Tell Their Story*, by Salvatore LaGumina. Copyright © 1979 by Salvatore LaGumina. Reprinted by permission of the Center for Migration Studies.

25 "Could We Ever Forget" by Ok Kork, translated by George Chigas, from *Cambodia's Lament: A Selection of Cambodian Poetry.* Copyright © 1991 by George Chigas. Reprinted by permission of George Chigas.

26 "Half Cuban" by Monique Rubio from *Hispanic, Female, and Young: An Anthology* edited by Phyllis Tashlik. Copyright © 1994 by Pinata Books, a division of Arte Publico Press-University of Houston. Reprinted by permission.

30 "How Everything Happens (Based on the Study of a Wave)" by May Swenson from *The Complete Poems to Solve.* Copyright © 1993 by The Literary Estate of May Swenson. Reprinted by permission of Macmillan Books for Young Readers, an imprint of Simon & Schuster Children's Publishing Division.

33 "At the Beach" by Kemal Ozer from *This Same Sky* translated by Dionis Riggs. Copyright © 1991 by Kemal Ozer. Reprinted by permission of Dionis Riggs.

35 "The Education of Berenice Belizaire" by Joe Klein from *Newsweek,* Aug. 9, 1993. Copyright © 1993 by *Newsweek,* Inc. All rights reserved. Reprinted by permission.

37 "West Side" from *Hugging the Jukebox* by Naomi Shihab Nye. Copyright © 1982 by Naomi Shihab Nye. Reprinted by permission of Breitenbush Books.

44 "Who's Hu?" by Lensey Namioka from *American Dragons* edited by Lawrence Yep. Copyright © 1980 by Lensey Namioka. Every attempt has been made to find the rights-holder of this article. If located, the rights-holder should contact Heinle & Heinle.

57 "Nicholasa Mohr" from *Speaking for Ourselves* edited by Donald R. Gallo. Copyright © 1994 by Nicholasa Mohr. Reprinted by permission of the author.

63 "The Underground Railroad" by Robert Peterson from *Boys' Life,* February 1993. Copyright © 1993 by Robert Peterson. Reprinted by permission of the author.

67 From *Take a Walk in Their Shoes* by Glennette Tilley Turner. Copyright © 1989 by Glennette Tilley Turner. Used by permission of Cobblehill Books, an affiliate of Dutton Children's Books, a division of Penguin USA, Inc.

73 "The Road Not Taken" by Robert Frost from *Mountain Interval,* 1916, Henry Holt and Co.

75 "Jessica Berg (Graduation)" by Mel Glenn from *Class Dismissed II.* Copyright © 1986 by Mel Glenn. Reprinted by permission of Clarion Books/Houghton Mifflin. All rights reserved.

78 "Footpath" by Stella Ngatho from *Poems of East Africa* edited by D. Cook and D. Rubadiri. Copyright © 1974. Every attempt has been made to find the rights-holder of this article. If located, the rights-holder should contact Heinle & Heinle.

79 "Harriet Tubman" from *Honey I Love* by Eloise Greenfield. Copyright © 1978 by Eloise Greenfield. Reprinted by permission of HarperCollins and Eloise Greenfield.

86 "Zoo" by Edward D. Hoch from *Young Extraterrestrials* edited by Martin Greenberg and Charles Waugh. Copyright © 1958 by King-Size Publications. Copyright © 1984 by Nightfall, Inc. Every attempt has been made to find the rights-holder of this article. If located, the rights-holder should contact Heinle & Heinle.